THE HISTORY OF UK BUSINESS AND MANAGEMENT EDUCATION

THE HISTORY OF UK BUSINESS AND MANAGEMENT EDUCATION

By

ALLAN P. O. WILLIAMS

Emeritus Professor
Cass Business School, City University London, UK

In conjunction with the Association of Business Schools

United Kingdom • North America • Japan
India • Malaysia • China

Emerald Group Publishing Limited
Howard House, Wagon Lane, Bingley BD16 1WA, UK

First edition 2010

British Library Cataloguing in Publication Data
A catalogue record for this book is available from the British Library

ISBN: 978-1-84950-780-6

Emerald Group Publishing
Limited, Howard House,
Environmental Management
System has been certified by
ISOQAR to ISO 14001:2004
standards

Awarded in recognition of
Emerald's production
department's adherence to
quality systems and processes
when preparing scholarly
journals for print

INVESTOR IN PEOPLE

Contents

Foreword

Business schools have been one of the great success stories of British higher education over the past 60 years. From the end of the Second World War formal business and management education in the United Kingdom expanded from being a marginal activity undertaken in a few dedicated institutions to become the single largest area of teaching and research in British universities. Today there are close to 150 business schools and other providers of business and management higher education in the United Kingdom. Among this large and growing number of business schools 117 are members of the Association of Business Schools (ABS). This book charts the development of these institutions and the subject area within which the staff of these schools have taught, researched and engaged in consultancy.

The idea for a history of business schools in the United Kingdom was born at a lunch given in honour of companions of the ABS in 2008. ABS Companions are elected by members of the Association in recognition of the work they have done to develop business and management education in the United Kingdom. At the first lunch Professor Sir George Bain, former chair of Warwick Business School and principal of London Business School, regaled the assembled collection business school deans with stories of his arrival in the United Kingdom in the late 1940s following time spent in the Canadian Merchant Navy during the Second World War. George told of the time he spent as a researcher at the University of Oxford and as a lecturer, professor and school chair at the University of Warwick, as well as time as the Principal at London Business School and most recently as Vice-Chancellor of Queens University Belfast. As this story unfolded, a parallel and often hidden story emerged of the development of university-based business and management education in the United Kingdom. Among George's humorous anecdotes and many changes of location the constant that emerged was the steady growth of a new subject area and of a range of institutions which had increasingly come to adopt the form of a business school.

In the discussion that followed George's talk at the ABS companions' lunch, many of those present told similar stories of developments in their own institutions. Fired up by these tales, George challenged Jonathan Slack and his colleagues at the ABS to compile a history of university-based business and management education. This book is the result of that challenge and of the hard work and dedication of the book's author, Allan Williams. Allan, who as emeritus professor at Cass Business School at City University London, has devoted many long hours to reading all of the published histories of business and management schools in the United Kingdom. A great number have been published over the course of the past 10 years as some of the founding fathers and mothers of university-based business and management education in the United Kingdom have slipped into semi-retirement and collected together their thoughts on developments over the past 40 years or more. In addition to reading these published and celebratory accounts, Allan also spent many days tracking down and talking to the deans and professors who have led or who currently lead major business schools in the United Kingdom.

In 2007, two years before taking on the task of writing a history of British business schools, Allan produced an impressive short history of the ABS to mark its fifteenth anniversary. In this current book he returns, extends and develops the points he made in that earlier history. As he demonstrates, the roots of university-based business and management education in the United Kingdom can be traced to the end of the nineteenth century and beginning of the twentieth century when professional associations were founded in Britain to aid the development of accountants, personnel managers, marketers and other nascent groups of generalist and specialist managers. Although formal business and management education at that time was an established feature of higher education in many parts of mainland Europe and the United States, early experiments with this type of education in the United Kingdom generally failed to develop the scale and acceptance from business people which would have been needed if they were to survive and prosper. Indeed, it was not until after the Second World War that formal business and management education began to develop more fully in the United Kingdom; and at this time, only in dedicated institutions which stood outside the established universities. The need to reconstruct a war-damaged economy and concern about low levels of productivity and competitiveness in the United Kingdom provided the spur for the first of a series of collective efforts by British business people and politicians to invest in the development of the knowledge, skills and other capabilities of aspiring and practising British managers. Over the next 30 years a number of new management colleges (i.e. Henley and Ashridge), business schools (i.e. London and Manchester) and university management departments (i.e. Cardiff, Lancaster and Warwick) were established or grew out of pre-existing commercial and technical colleges or polytechnics (e.g. Aston, Bath, Kingston, Loughbrough and Regents Street Polytechnic). In these institutions undergraduate and postgraduate education developed through the launch of new courses, including the Certificate and Diploma in Management Studies, Higher National Certificate and Diploma, as well as the BA Business Studies. Alongside these new post-experience and undergraduate courses were added masters in management, the MBA and a growing range of more specialist undergraduate and postgraduate courses in the 1980s and 1990s. Over this period PhD courses in business and management also became more important as route to qualification for people drawn into careers in business and management higher education and research.

Today in 2010 after 60 years of relentless development and growth, there are over 250,000 full-time equivalent students studying business and management at foundation, undergraduate, postgraduate taught and postgraduate research levels in publicly funded universities in the United Kingdom. These students, together with the 20,000 or more students studying in privately funded institutions, constitute 15% of the total complement of higher education students in the United Kingdom. They also account for the lion's share of international students studying in the United Kingdom and for many more students studying overseas under licence from a UK university. The business and management education these students receive enables them to work more effectively and efficiently in a range of companies, public sector agencies and voluntary organizations in an increasingly globalized world. It also contributes to the export performance of the United Kingdom through earning many millions of pounds of foreign currency.

As the student numbers in British business schools have grown over the past 60 years, so have the number of staff employed to teach them and to undertake the research- and enterprise-related activities which generate new knowledge, challenge established conventions and help to develop new products, services, processes and organizations. In 2010 there are over 11,000 business and management academic staff employed in publicly funded universities in the United Kingdom and at least a further 1000 academic staff employed in privately funded institutions. Of these staff approximately 75% were employed in permanent full-time positions and 25% on temporary and part-time contracts.

Growth in the number of academic staff working in the field of business and management studies has not been relentless but it has not been constant. In the period immediately after the Second World War there were less than 10 professors working in subject areas which might today be considered to be the forerunners of modern business and management studies. Today there are over 3000 research active staff in UK business schools of whom close to 1000 are professors in business and management of a related subject area. Growth in the numbers of these staff and in the range of activities they perform has happened in spurts and splutters. In the immediate post-war period reliance on funding from private sector companies and individuals limited the rate of growth although corporate donors through various collective bodies provided the capital and investment in staff training needed for some of the first business schools and regional management centres. It was not until the massive expansion in higher education from the mid-1960s till the mid-1970s that staff numbers became clear. Then from the mid-1970s until the mid-1980s successive recessions and restrictions on public spending limited the scope for universities to employ new staff and to train the next generation of academics. It was only really in the period between the late 1980s and end of the first decade of the twenty-first century that massive expansion in numbers took place, fuelled by significant increases in public sector spending and rapid increases in the number of overseas students wishing to study business and management in UK-based universities. As a consequence of language, location and perhaps most importantly high value for money, the United Kingdom remains the second most popular destination for overseas higher education students in the world.

As the number of staff involved in teaching and researching business and management has expanded over recent years so have the range of specialisms which make up this subject area. Over the past 50 years, the founding social science disciplines of economics, psychology, sociology and law have been extended, developed or dropped to be replaced by business environment, organization studies, consumer behaviour and strategy. These subject areas have in turn been built upon by advances in research and scholarship within the functional core curriculum areas of accounting, finance, information systems, marketing, operations management, human resource management and international business, as well as a myriad of specialisms which build on these cores, focus on the specific contexts within which they are practised or, as in the case of business ethics and sustainability, cross-cut all aspects of commercial activity.

While the curriculum of business and management higher education has grown and developed significantly over the past 50 years it appears in retrospect that a few areas of contemporary practice may have been overlooked by the increasing number of specialist conferences, journals and textbooks which support academic research and teaching. Among the areas which may be missing are local and regional political economy, construction and facilities management, intellectual property rights, health and safety, sales, export and trade.

The tradition of established disciplines and specialisms within business and management provides a supportive hand for the many individuals who work within these subject areas in business schools across the country. It also, on occasion, lays a heavy hand on future developments. The isomorphic forces of subject benchmark standards, accreditation schemes, newspaper league tables and management development programmes for business school academics provide powerful encouragement for individuals keen to develop and steer their own careers. However, they also may encourage these same individuals and the institutions within which they work to behave in very similar ways. Ironically, it would seem that at a time when business schools have been identified as the sites within which reflexive management has been encouraged and the mechanisms of capitalisms have become better known, and knowing (Thrift, 2005) the relentless pursuit of shareholder value through textbook solutions may have blinded us to the limits of markets, growth and profit (Centeno & Cohen, 2010).

In the summer of 2010, the British economy has emerged from 18 months of recession and stands ready for future economic growth in the private sector while large parts of the public sector, including the country's universities, look set for cuts in their activities. The combination of these cuts in university funding, together with concern about the economic, social and environmental contribution of business schools looks set to alter the size, shape and form of business and management education in the United Kingdom over the next five years. As deans, professors, lecturers and students in these institutions consider how best to negotiate these challenges and the pressures of increased competition from private sector institutions and overseas providers, this history of business schools in the United Kingdom provides an excellent basis for understanding how the present constellation of institutions developed. As the themes and strands in this history demonstrate, the current form was not inevitable. Many different ideas and events have played a part in the development of this industry and doubtless many more, as yet unforeseen, ideas and events will play a part in future developments. As we prepare for this future this book helps us to understand where we are and most importantly where we came from.

The book is a tribute to the hard work of Allan Williams who researched, wrote and compiled it and a testament to the many business school academics who have built a great industry.

References

Centeno, M., & Cohen, J. (2010). *Global capitalism: A sociological perspective.* Cambridge: Polity Press.
Thrift, N. (2005). *Knowing capitalism.* London: Sage.

Huw Morris
Howard Thomas
Chair of ABS and
Immediate Past Chair of ABS

Introduction

One of the outstanding educational phenomena occurring in the latter half of the past century is the growth of the business school industry in the United Kingdom. The publication of the Franks Report in 1963 is generally recognized as a milestone in this development. But the historical roots can be traced back many more years. Figure 0.1 is a framework around which to organize our historical observations. It conveys the complex dynamic relationships between the major elements that are central to achieving the aims of this publication, i.e. a readable and reliable account of the emergence of business and management education in the United Kingdom, with particular emphasis on business schools.

Organizations have to be led and managed. The challenge is to do this in an environment that is continually changing, and where organizations find themselves competing for scarce resources and discerning customers. Organizations come in various shapes and sizes, and they import different resources, export different products and services and operate in different

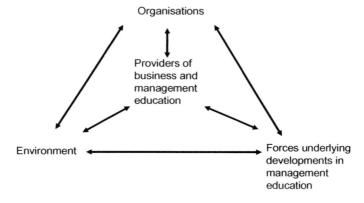

Fig. 0.1: The rise of business and management education in the United Kingdom: model of the basic elements.

markets and cultures. Moreover, the *environment* contains a whole host of factors that impinge on their performance, including political and social, economic, technological, and scientific. Leading and managing in such complex organization–environmental (O/E) systems require relevant *business and management knowledge and skills*. It is therefore no surprise to find that as the competitive climate increased, organizations found that learning on the job had to be supplemented by formal training to ensure the acquisition of relevant knowledge and skills. This need has resulted in the gradual emergence of the *providers of business and management education* (e.g. professional institutions, educational institutions and consultancies).

Chapter 1 identifies key individuals, events and forces in the historical development of business and management education (henceforth abbreviated to management education). It includes the early formation of the professional bodies associated with management (e.g. Chartered Institute of Personnel and Development (CIPD) and Chartered Management Institute (CMI)), and the early academic interventions of the London School of Economics (LSE) and Manchester and Birmingham universities. A milestones chart is introduced to help the reader trace key historical sequences. Chapter 2 focuses on bodies representing and regulating UK business schools (e.g. Association of Business Schools (ABS) and Association of MBAs (AMBA)). Their emergence has been the result of the extraordinary growth of this sector of higher education, and the accompanying need to set and maintain quality standards in relation to qualifications and institutions. Chapter 3 focuses on the generation and dissemination of knowledge that has formed the cornerstone of management education in the United Kingdom, i.e. the research institutions, programmes and authors that have influenced thinking in this area, and therefore what is taught and how it is taught. The historical roles of academic bodies such as the Tavistock Institute of Human Relations, the Association of Teachers of Management and the British Academy of Management (BAM) are touched upon; as are other UK learned societies and publications linked to management education. Chapter 4 looks at the nature and composition of ABS members (as the body representing all UK business schools) and their standing relative to business schools worldwide. Brief case studies are included of a sample of schools in an attempt to illustrate the similarities and diversities involved in the birth and development of these business schools. By way of conclusion Chapter 5 presents a dynamic model which draws together the main forces that have driven the historical development of management education in the United Kingdom. Within the context of this model the role of 'leadership' in initiating and maintaining the coping responses of organizations are highlighted.

Chapter 1

Historical Overview of UK Business and Management Education

1.1. Introduction

One of the first tasks in researching this history was to trawl through those publications where distinguished scholars had identified the institutions and individuals relevant to our enquiry (e.g. Brech, 2000, 2002; Wilson & Thomson, 2006). The reliability of this initial list was further tested by interviewing a number of senior figures in UK business schools, as well as a number of experts who had researched and published in this field (see acknowledgements in Appendix 1). The milestones arrived at after several revisions are listed in Box 1.2.

How can such a chronological list be interpreted so as to reveal a linked and readable narrative of the significant developments leading to the present scene? The structure adopted is to divide the story into five sub-themes: the emergence of early networks and pressure groups; professional bodies associated with management; academia's early interventions; the influence of the Foundation for Management Education (FME); management consultancies and corporate universities. This structure is not intended to undermine the value of the change-enabling forces generated by several reports/publications in the development of management education in the United Kingdom.

1.2. The Emergence of Early Networks and Pressure Groups

Individuals sharing common objectives, and facing similar problems, are likely to form informal networks enabling them to learn from one another. If the mutual rewards are sufficiently great, these networks eventually become formalized into a legal body such as an association. Formalization enables such groups to be recognized as representing particular sectors in the community or economy. In other words, they become potential pressure groups to protect and promote the interests of their members in the wider environment.

In the late eighteenth and nineteenth centuries much of the knowledge and skills for success in manufacturing and commerce rested on apprenticeship systems, work experience and networking. A number of formal bodies emerged that facilitated learning. Thus, the *Society for the Encouragement of Arts, Manufactures and Commerce* (*RSA*) was founded in 1754. The Society was founded by William Shipley, a drawing master living in Northampton, to 'support improvements in the liberal arts and sciences, and to stimulate enterprise for the common good'. The RSA initiated the Great Exhibition of 1851. According to its delegates the success of that exhibition was not replicated at the Paris International Exposition of 1867. This perceived gap led to a number of educational initiatives although, as Brech points out, the cause for the gap was thought to be the technical rather than the managerial deficiencies of engineers. The RSA is still active today. Indeed in 1993 it brought together 25 of the United Kingdom's top businesses under the leadership of Sir Anthony Cleaver, Chairman of IBM UK, to develop a shared vision of Tomorrow's Company (RSA, 1995). The objective was to stimulate greater competitive performance by encouraging UK business leaders, and those who influence their decision-making, to re-examine the sources of sustainable success.

The present *British Chambers of Commerce* (*BCC*) is a powerful network of Chambers of Commerce across the United Kingdom. These bodies exist to support local/national businesses, and are a source of representation, information and guidance. Many local chambers of commerce emerged during the latter half of the eighteenth century, and they came together to form the Association of Chambers of Commerce in 1861. The learning potential of the BCC is evident from the published account of its 240 years history (Taylor, 2007).

The Confederation of British Industry (*CBI*) emerged in 1965 from a group of older employers' organizations: the Federation of British Industries (FBI), the British Employers' Confederation and the National Association of British Manufacturers. They all aimed at influencing economic decisions taken by governments. The CBI has become a very powerful lobbying group on behalf of employers. Since the CBI's mission is to help create and sustain the conditions in which businesses in the United Kingdom can compete and prosper for the benefit of all, it is no surprise to find that it has influenced events in the development of business and management education in the United Kingdom (e.g. Franks Report).

1.3. Professional Bodies Associated with Management

In the middle and latter half of the nineteenth century, the term 'engineering' was increasingly being used, and this was reinforced in 1847 with the formation of the *Institution of Mechanical Engineers* and the publication of regular journals devoted to engineering. Its primary purpose when founded was 'to give an impulse to inventions likely to be useful to the world'; syllabuses relating to organization and management were introduced into their qualifications in the early twentieth century.

As Brech (2000) points out, major commercial ventures (e.g. railway systems) brought about a growth in financial partnerships which led to the 'company' legislation in 1855–1862, and to the emergence of accountancy associations. Several of these formed *The Institute of Chartered Accountants* in 1880, and from this date accountancy took the form of an organized profession with the granting of a Royal Charter in 1880, and subsequently with the setting of standards of professional conduct. The profession has grown primarily as a result of the commercial and legal activity of bankruptcy, insolvency and the winding up of companies. It is interesting to note that the first application for membership by a woman was turned down in 1888, and that in 1909 the President of the Board of Trade (Winston Churchill) requested that women should be admitted (www.icaew.com). In the same year the first woman accountant was admitted, but many aspects of the male culture persisted even as recently as 1979 (Silverstone & Williams, 1979). In Scotland the accountancy bodies attached to the main cities merged to form the Institute of Chartered Accountants of Scotland in 1951. An attempt by the Institute of Chartered Accountants for England and Wales (ICAEW) — a title used since 1880 — in 1968 to merge the various accountancy bodies failed. Today the ICAEW is one of the largest professional bodies in Europe with 132,000 members running and advising businesses across all economic sectors and counts the majority of the FT Stock Exchange (FTSE) CEOs and Finance Directors as members. The Institute undertakes or facilitates a wide range of professional activities including education and training of students, continuing professional development for members, maintenance of professional and ethical standards, cutting-edge work on technical accounting issues, and provision of advice and services to members.

Although towards the second half of the nineteenth century there was little sign of demands for 'management' education as such, the education theme for occupational groups was taking root as a source of efficiency and competitive standing. A conference in 1875, organized by the Corporation of London and the Livery Companies, led in 1879 to the creation of *The City and Guilds of London Institute*. In 1889 government legislation enabled local authorities to spend public funds on educational facilities, and the resulting technical colleges brought about the formation of the *Association of Technical Institutions* in 1894. Further developments in the direction of occupational studies and examinations were displayed in the formation of new bodies such as the *Chartered Institute of Secretaries* in 1902. The Companies Acts of 1900–1901 (which created new liabilities for members of boards of directors) encouraged the formation of an *Institute of Directors* (*IOD*) in 1903. In 1906 it received its Royal Charter. Today the IOD is Europe's largest membership organization for senior level business professionals, and offers its members an influential network of colleagues, advisory and professional development programmes, as well as an industry-recognized qualification — Chartered Director.

The start-up of three other professional bodies closely linked to management education should be highlighted. What is now known as the *Chartered Institute of Marketing* (*CIM*) began life as the Sales Managers' Association in 1911. This Association was created to improve sales techniques and to set the role of sales on a more professional footing. The Association's aims were 'To promote, encourage and coordinate the study and advancement of sales management in all its branches, both home and overseas. To initiate and maintain investigation and research into the best methods of sales management, to safeguard the interests of sales managers, to extend, increase and disseminate knowledge, to exchange information and ideas with regard to all matters concerned therewith, and to assist and further, in all practicable ways, the development and improvement of sales management, market research, advertising and the conduct and handling of all sales of commodities, goods and services in the higher interest of the British People'. In subsequent years, the Association's name changed to the Incorporated Sales Managers' Association (ISMA) in 1921, and one of the early developments was the formation of a library (500 books available by 1924). In 1928 the first annual certificate examinations were held, and in 1931 the ISMA magazine was renamed 'Marketing' to underline the journal's importance in the business sciences. Its notable contribution to the Second World War was the innovative correspondence courses for service personnel (at one time examinations involving 6000 students were held in 82 prisoner of war camps). In 1961, changes in the industry led the Association to change its name to The Institute of Marketing and Sales Management. In the same year the Association's examination was reintroduced as the Diploma in Marketing. During the National Productivity Year of 1963, the government stressed the importance of marketing as the essential element in improving UK business performance. Another name change was made in 1968 to The Institute of Marketing. In 1973, members were required to observe the Institute's first Code of Practice.

In 1989, it was awarded a Royal Charter at the third attempt (previous ones were in 1936 and 1982). Hence, the current label of the Chartered Institute of Marketing. Its governing principles as set out in the Royal

Charter include: '... to promote and develop the art and science of marketing and to encourage, advance and disseminate knowledge, education and practical training in and research into that art and science'. It is worth noting that in 1992 the European Union adopted the Institute's Diploma as the preferred professional marketing qualification through member states. In 1994, the Diploma was recognized as a postgraduate qualification. The national standing of the Institute was recognized in 2001 when the Department of Education and Skills asked it to develop world-class benchmarks of best practice for marketing.

The current *Chartered Institute of Personnel and Development* (*CIPD*) started life in 1913 as the Welfare Workers' Association. In the interval between 1917 and 1946 (when the Institute of Personnel Management (IPM) title was in use) several name changes occurred. The Institute of Personnel and Development was introduced in 1994 on the amalgamation of the IPM and the Institute of Training and Development. The latter had started life as the British Association for Commercial Education in 1919 with the aim of ensuring suitable training and education was provided for those entering industry and commerce; in 1934 it amalgamated with the Association for Education in Industry and Commerce to form the British Association for Commercial and Industrial Education (BACIE). The present name followed the granting of the Royal Charter in 2000. The CIPD sees itself as the professional body for those involved in the management and development of people. Since the early 1920s a body of knowledge began to be accumulated which was relevant for personnel managers. In more recent years the institute developed educational qualifications which their members were expected to possess for employment as a personnel manager. These qualifications could be run internally or by higher education bodies whose corresponding qualifications had been accredited by the institute. For many years the institute has had an active research and publication function, particularly as a commissioner of research projects based in universities (Williams, Dobson et al., 1989).

A major professional body that requires highlighting is the *Chartered Management Institute* (*CMI*). Its current vision is 'First-class management and leadership driving up personal and corporate performance, national productivity and social well being'. To achieve this mission the institute promotes the art and science of management to 'encourage and support the lifelong development of managers; raise the level of competence and qualification of management; initiate, develop, evaluate and disseminate management thinking, tools, techniques and practices; influence employers, policy makers and opinion formers on management issues'. It was in 1920 that a precursor body was brought into being as the Institute of Industrial Administration on the initiative of Elbourne, who 'recognized the need for managers to have specific professional education and training'. However, the institute ceased functioning in 1924 (but see below) and as Brech points out it was left to others to progress the thinking and objectives of Elbourne (Brech, 2000). For example, the Association for Advancement of Education in Industry and Commerce brought together directors and managers from the larger companies and educational personnel in 1919. This was originally intended to facilitate the transition of school leavers entering employment but it then focused on the education and development of supervisory and managerial responsibilities. In 1947, a younger branch came into being as the British Institute of Management (BIM). Four years later the two bodies merged, but it was only in 1957 that full integration took place.

Two stalwarts in the management education field were Seebohm Rowntree and Lyndall Urwick. One of several initiatives they took was the setting up of the Management Research Groups (MRG) in 1926. These groups were located in various parts of the country, and were forums for the exchange of knowledge and know-how relating to management. The MRG Council invited Urwick to draft a proposal and a constitution for a British institute of management. Although he submitted it in 1930, it did not attract sufficient support from powerful bodies to move it forward. However, a meeting convened by the Board of Trade in 1944 agreed that a 'British Institute of Management should be initiated and supported by Government'. In 1945, the Baillieu Committee was set up by the Board of Trade to consider this issue, and the BIM was formed in 1947 (Baillieu, 1945). Since the Baillieu Committee did not favour the integration of related bodies (e.g. Institute of Industrial Administration) in the new organization, the full representation of the BIM took another 10 years to come about.

In 1945, a committee to review management education was established by the Board of Trade and chaired by Lyndall Urwick. By 1947 a national scheme was agreed for a management qualification, and the Diploma in Management Studies (DMS) was launched over the period 1949–1952 by the BIM and the Ministry of Education. This was a first in terms of a management qualification in academia, and a precursor of the later 'imported' Master of Business Administration (MBA) degrees.

Another initiative of the Board of Trade was the establishment of *The British Productivity Council (BPC)* in 1952. This came about as a result of the success of the Anglo-American Productivity Programme to accumulate and disseminate managerial knowledge and know-how to companies and educational centres (Mace, 1952). In Brech's opinion the BPC did more for managerial advancement during the 1950s and 1960s than the BIM (Brech, 2000).

In more recent years the role of the BIM (now CMI) has been significant. In 1975, the MRG were absorbed into the BIM. In 1987 and subsequent years BIM joined other bodies to sponsor two highly influential studies (Constable & McCormick, 1987; Handy, Gordon et al., 1987), and became involved in the implementation of some of their recommendations. One of these was the creation of the National Forum for Management Education and Development (NFMED) in 1988. 'The NFMED was established in 1988 with backing from BP, IBM, Shell and the government. Its aim was to act as a catalyst for change through increasing interest in, and attention paid to, management development. The Management Charter Initiative (MCI) was its operational and marketing arm' (IM, 1994, p. 26). The MCI issued a set of competency-based national management standards to be used as a basis for Certificates and Diplomas awarded by various awarding bodies. Their definition of 'competence' means the ability to perform effectively the functions associated with management in a work-related situation. The competence approach has yielded mixed results, particularly within the context of universities and their business schools. The latter rejected the approach partly due to the difficulty employers experienced in understanding the concept, and also because of the problem of using a competence framework which focused on the past in times of uncertainty and change, and undervalues knowledge and theory in management education (IM, 1994; Burgoyne, 1988).

In 1994, the institute, together with the Association of Business Schools (ABS), formed the Management Verification Consortium (MVC) to accredit the nationally recognized management vocational qualifications offered by the business schools in the United Kingdom. In 2000 the Institute launched its MBA, and two years later its management qualifications were recognized as part of the United Kingdom's National Qualifications Framework for Higher Education. In the same year the institute was granted a Royal Charter, and rebranded itself as the CMI.

Today the CMI is a significant player in management education. It is the leading body for professional management, and plays an important role in disseminating the latest insights and setting standards in management development. Its activities are geared to improving business performance. It carries out regular surveys of its 79,000 individual members and 480 corporate members, and these form the basis of a series of reports covering a wide range of relevant topics. For example, *Developing Managers: A European Perspective* (Mabey & Ramirez, 2004), a survey across seven countries showing that the United Kingdom was one of those spending less than the European mean on management development per manager per year; *The Value of Management Qualifications: The Perspective of UK Employers and Managers* (Wilton, Woodman et al., 2007), drawing attention to the fact that managers in the United Kingdom are significantly underqualified compared to other professional occupations, and that a literature review shows growing evidence that management qualifications impact positively on productivity; *Management Futures: The World in 2018* (CMI, 2008), contains the views of experts as to what the world of work would look like in 2018 and what business leaders need to do in order to prepare for this future scenario.

A 'professional' body in an early stage in its development has recently merged with the CMI. This is the *Institute of Business Consulting* (*IBC*) which aims to be the body for the consultancy profession. In 1961, an Institute of Management Consultants (IMC) was formed to deal with matters affecting the profession; the name was modified during the 1990s to Institute of Management Consultancy so as to attract corporate as well as individual members. In 2005, the IMC merged with the CMI, and soon after, the Institute of Business Counsellors (established in 1989, and operating primarily with owner/managers and small firms) merged with IMC. In 2007, the two consultancy bodies created the IBC within their host the CMI. The IBC is now the intended professional body for all business consultants and advisers. It aims to raise the standards of professional practice in support of better business performance, and to provide a recognized qualifications route. With the resources of the CMI it now has a better chance of achieving these aims.

There is a rich vein of professional bodies in the United Kingdom; a few more that have contributed to the commercial success of the country will be mentioned. The history of the *Chartered Insurance Institute* (*CII*) goes back to 1873 when the first insurance institute was founded in Manchester. In 1897, the various insurance institutes in the country were brought together into a federation; the federation was granted a Royal Charter in 1912, and took on the current name of the CII. In 1957, the CII opened a College of Insurance with courses having both a training and educational content. Today the Institute with its 90,000 members claims to be the premier professional organization for those working in the insurance and financial services industry; and dedicates itself to 'promoting higher standards of competence and integrity through the provision of relevant qualifications for employees at all levels and across all sectors'.

The *Chartered Institute of Bankers* was founded in 1879, but only incorporated by Royal Charter in 1987. Its mission statement is 'To be the leading provider of education to the financial services industry'. This was undoubtedly an outcome of the Wilde Committee, a working party appointed by the Institute in 1972 'to undertake a comprehensive review of the Institute's future role as a qualifying association' (Wilde, 1973). The Wilde Report heralded an extension of professionalism in banking, and advocated those 'who are likely to reach senior positions in their banks to start studying systematically the ways in which problems of management must be approached and decisions made'. In 1993 it merged with the Chartered Building Societies Institute, and in 1996 it established the Institute of Financial Services as a charitable trust to develop and deliver a range of appropriate qualifications (e.g. a Diploma in Financial Services

Management; an Associateship linked to the award of a BSc in Financial Services from the University of Manchester Institute of Science and Technology (UMIST)). It is also the awarding body for Financial Services National Vocational Qualifications (NVQs) for banks and building societies, covering the whole academic, professional and vocational spectrum. The Institute became active in publishing books linked to its qualifications. An example is *Management and People in Banking* which was first published in 1980. This covered a series of topics central to management, written by business school academics and banking practitioners (Livy, 1980).

The role of the professional bodies in the education of managers in the United Kingdom should not be underestimated. In the case of BIM/CMI its contribution is obvious, but this was hardly noticeable in its early years. It has been criticized for not grasping the nettle of management education by not taking an earlier responsibility for a recognized qualification in management (i.e. the DMS) as a prerequisite for practicing managers (Brech, 2002). A likely reason for this was that when the BIM was formed in 1947 as a result of the Baillieu Report, and with the financial support of the Board of Trade, there was an ideological clash between the Labour government of Attlee (and its interventionist policies) and Industry. The result was that the FBI tended to ignore the early days of the BIM and its DMS qualification (Larson, 2009).

The early history of other professional bodies mentioned above may not have specifically mentioned management education in their mission, but since the areas of knowledge covered are related to the disciplines underlying management their contributions to the effective practice of management are real. This 'indirect' contribution is clearly visible in the case of the bodies representing the accountancy profession as Matthews, Anderson et al. have shown in their paper from which the following information is drawn (1997). The number of qualified accountants working in Britain appears to have grown by 7–9% per annum from 1882 to 1911, and subsequently fell to a steady rate of 3–4%. 'Accountancy has been by far the fastest growing of the major professions in Britain in the past century, out-distancing doctors, lawyers, teachers, and engineers/scientists'. Before 1918, accountants were mainly employed as professional practitioners, but in the inter-war years and subsequently an increasing number took up full-time employment in business. Just 3% worked outside practice in 1911, but just under two-thirds by 1991. Between 1891 and 1911 few accountants held senior positions in business; by 1991 more than one-fifth of all directors were accountants. 'Moreover, in this process of the professionalization of company boards accountants took a clear lead. ... Until 1931, the most popular "qualification" of board members in Britain was a noble title; next frequent was a military title. Professional qualifications were scarce, and very few directors of listed companies had degrees. Professional qualifications were on the increase from the 1930s, and equally noticeable is the extent to which accountants were in the ascendant, being by 1991 twice as numerous on British boards of directors as lawyers and engineers put together' (Matthews, Anderson et al., 1997, p. 411).

In trying to explain these historical observations on accountancy Matthews et al. put forward various explanations, including the Companies Act of 1900 making compulsory the auditing of all limited companies, managers needing more information for the internal control of their companies in the context of increasing expansion and mergers, and so on. Particularly relevant are the authors' comments as to why professionally trained accountants moved so noticeably into general management. The need for good financial advice during the problems facing the British economy was the obvious reason; but their preferred explanation was the quality of the recruits to the profession combined with the 'fact that, until recently, the accountants' articles were virtually the only formal management training available in Britain'. In other words, many talented individuals entered accountancy as a pathway to a business career. Britain's major competitors had the alternative routes of university degrees together with corporate training for their managers. Statistics available throughout the twentieth century show that the proportion of graduates in management in the United Kingdom was far less than those in the United States, Germany and Japan; also, for most of the century in-company management training was the exception rather than the rule. It was this vacuum that was partially filled by accountants before the growth of the business school industry in the United Kingdom. From the early days 'young accountants also studied law, and from 1922 had the option of economics, banking, or actuarial science' (Matthews, Anderson et al., 1997).

There are signs that professional bodies associated with management are aspiring to develop into a significant 'pressure group'. Eight of them commissioned London Economics (Chapman, Conlon et al., 2008) to carry out research examining how professional bodies can contribute to the national Skills Strategy associated with the Leitch Report (Leitch, 2006). The eight concerned are as follows: Chartered Institute of Logistics and Transport (20,000 members in 30 countries); Chartered Institute of Management Accountants (164,000 members and students in 161 countries); CIM (47,000 members worldwide); CIPD (130,000 members); Chartered Institute of Purchasing and Supply (50,000 members in 140 countries); CMI (71,500 individual and group members); Institute of Credit Management; Institute of Chartered Secretaries and Administrators (36,000 members in 70 countries).

This informal body was formed 'in recognition of the fact that the current infrastructure for skills — driven by sector and regional priorities — makes inadequate provision for supporting the higher level business skills that are critical to all sectors and regions'. In support of their impact, the Consultative Committee for Professional Management Organisations

(CCPMO) is able to claim to provide over 50,000 professional awards a year, focused on the business and management professions, to show that employers place a high value on the skills provided and to draw attention to associated activities that benefit the incidence of high-quality professional activity to the benefit of the economy — e.g. research development, knowledge dissemination and policy development.

1.4. Academia's Early Interventions

In the United Kingdom the end of the nineteenth and beginning of the twentieth centuries saw the first tentative attempts of academia to enter the management education field. It is generally recognized that the first business school in the United States was Wharton when it was established in 1881, and it remains today one of the top schools in the world. The oldest school in France was founded in 1819 under the name 'Ecole Speciale de Commerce et d'Industrie' by a group of Parisian businessmen and intellectuals, and remains one of the top schools in Europe (Servan-Schreiber, 1994). For many reasons the United Kingdom lagged behind these countries. One reason often given is the belief, held by many owners of businesses, CEOs and government officials that management/leadership performance is due to inherited abilities; education and training can only make a minor contribution. This view prevailed in the nineteenth and, to a lesser extent, in the first half of the twentieth centuries.

Several UK universities claim to be the first to introduce administrative and commercial education in their curricula. It is far from an exact science to identify exactly when a university entered the field; this is largely due to the mélange of subjects involved. In 1902, there was a Faculty of Commerce in the *University of Birmingham* with a professor and a bachelor degree. *Manchester University* established a Faculty of Commerce in 1903 'to meet the specific needs of young men who intended a career in private enterprise'. With a general curriculum consisting of political economy, some law, accountancy and optional subjects, the new faculty in fact began to recruit both men and women (the latter slowly at first). The intention had always been to prepare for a career in public administration as well as in business; this wish became a reality in 1927 when it was renamed the Faculty of Commerce and Administration and began to award degrees in Commerce and Administration (Moore, 2007). However, in Dahrendorf's history of the *London School of Economics* (*LSE*) he refers to one of the founders, Sidney Webb, describing the LSE in 1897 as 'the beginning of a High School of Commerce' (Dahrendorf, 1995, p. 59). He then refers to a 1901 report published by its director, William Hewins, where the following mission appears: 'The conception of Higher Commercial Education adopted by the

School was that a system of higher education especially adapted to the needs of the "captains of industry and commerce", a system, that is, which provides scientific training in the structure and organization of modern industry and commerce, and the general causes and criteria of prosperity, as these are illustrated or explained in the policy and the experience of the British Empire and foreign countries' (Hewins, 1901). In Dahrendorf's view the 'High School of Commerce' is nothing other than a business school in modern parlance. In 1917, Sidney Webb (then Professor of Public Administration in the University of London) published a booklet in which he declared 'Management becoming conscious of itself as a distinct profession' (Brech, 2000). In 1921, the University of London invested the Prince of Wales (later Edward VIII and then Duke of Windsor) with the degrees DSc and MCom at the time when the new degrees in Commerce were being launched. But the BCom and MCom degrees were never a great success, and were eventually abolished in 1954 (Harte, 1986).

There is one more pioneering effort that should be mentioned. The Institute of Mechanical Engineers had included a syllabus relating to workshop organization and management into their qualification, and this was introduced in 1925 at the *Regent Street Polytechnic* (now the University of Westminster). In 1925 Elbourne had completed his Institute of Industrial Administration professional studies, and in 1928 he saw an opportunity of introducing it as a part-time evening course at the Polytechnic, given its enterprising nature. All participants were post-experience and the programme required three years of attendance. The Institute's syllabus was recognized as optional by the engineering institutions in 1932, thus helping in the revival of the Institute of Industrial Administration.

In 1937, a new body was formed to provide a national managerial coordinating focus — the British Management Council. One of its early tasks was to review the nation's existing educational facilities for the study of management, and to identify the common elements of management knowledge and practice underlying the four functions of 'labour, office, purchasing and works (manufacturing)'. The publication of their endeavours had to be postponed because of the outbreak of the Second World War. After the war the British Management Council gave way to the BIM.

1.5.   The Influence of the Foundation for Management Education

The early 1960s saw the start of a remarkable phenomenon in business and management education in the United Kingdom — the creation of university-based business schools. The only institution that came close to this concept before those years was the Administrative Staff College at Henley. The college was established in 1946, and launched its first courses in 1948 (Rundle, 2006). It was the first British institution focusing on the training of managers and administrators for greater responsibility.

Two influential reports in 1963 brought together a number of forces that gave impetus to the development of the business school: the Robbins Report (Robbins, 1963) and the Franks Report (Franks, 1963). The former paved the way for the expansion of management schools in the higher education and polytechnic sector; the latter ensured that business and management education made inroads in the university sector. Both developments were helped by the formation of the FME in 1960. FME played a pivotal role for many years in the development of business schools in the United Kingdom, and therefore requires special attention (Box 1.1).

This was the opening paragraph of Philip Nind's story of the FME (he was the second Director, from 1968 to 1983). It was worth quoting because it shows that major forces behind the business and management education movement came about through the influence of powerful individuals in industry and commerce rather than from the initiatives of academia. A reason for this was that the impetus came from the perceived need in the

---

Box 1.1.   The birth of the FME.

'FME was born in 1960, the outcome of two years of discussion by a small group of men who met at regular intervals at the House of Commons in the fervent belief that management was a field of intellectual endeavour which should be encouraged and fostered at British universities in the urgent interest of the nation's economic and industrial performance. These founding fathers included, amongst others, two businessmen Members of Parliament, Sir Keith Joseph ... and Sir John Rodgers; Sir Peter Parker, then of Booker Brothers; John L. Smith of Coutts and Royal Exchange Assurance; Sir Hugh Tett of Esso; James Platt of Shell; Sir Keith Murray, Chairman of the University Grants Committee; Sir Noel Hall, founder Principal of the Administrative Staff College Henley; and, in the light of the thought he has given to the subject since the late 1940s and of the time and effort he has devoted to British management education as Chairman of FME since 1968 and in many other ways, the *primus inter pares*, John Bolton, who is himself a graduate (MBA) of the Harvard Business School. Most of these were businessmen and it was indeed from industry and commerce that the impetus for the "take-off" of university management education was to come' (Nind 1985, p. 1).

United Kingdom to improve productivity after the Second World War, and the belief that the higher productivity of the United States was partly due to the success of their business schools. The extract also shows how the early experience of an individual (e.g. John Bolton) can be a determining factor in later developments. The group forming FME were firm believers that the controversy as to whether managers are born or made was a side issue, what was important is that management can be made better through education and training.

An initial attempt to interest one or two universities to introduce courses in management resulted in Cambridge coming forward with a proposal for a postgraduate course to be available to their scientists and engineers (April 1959). Two other proposals came from Bristol and Leeds. A few companies promised funds so that grants could be made for these courses (including £35,000 from John Bolton of Solartron). Some companies made it clear that they would not support proposals for undergraduate or postgraduate courses in management (e.g. Vickers). An important addition to the Group was the ex-Shell managing director, James Platt who was a strong believer in management education at university level. In 1960, he was appointed by the Government to the post of Chairman of the UK Advisory Council on Education for Management.

In their fund-raising campaign, the Group stressed the need for industry to demonstrate to Government and to the universities its support for management courses. They stressed the complexity over which managers would have to operate in the future, and the need for universities to advance relevant knowledge. They used the analogy of the medical profession to show how universities had established a fruitful relationship between thinkers and practitioners; and foresaw a similar relationship being developed in management. They were not promoting the idea of training in practical techniques but rather the concern should be 'with studies in depth in aspects of certain fields of knowledge which contribute to an understanding of the problems of business organization and management — disciplines such as the social sciences, the human sciences, and mathematics' (Nind, 1985, p. 13). In time they foresaw a new discipline developing from the relationship between management studies and these fields of study; research was an important ingredient in this process.

Attention was drawn to the support of the University Grants Committee (UGC) by quoting from its 1957 quinquennial report 'the development of management as an academic discipline represents a worthwhile challenge, in facing which industry and commerce, as well as the universities, have an important part to play'. However, the universities required to be convinced before entering the management education field. University-based management education was still only accepted by some companies and some universities! In the summer of 1960 the Group formed a legal entity as the

FME. In order to continue supporting projects already committed to, and to consider new requests, the FME had to make further appeals and work closely with the UGC. The latter set up a special panel to consider the new proposals that FME was attracting. In May 1963 the Government agreed to share with FME the financing of nine universities for projects in management studies.

Philip Nind refers to 1963 as a momentous year 'in which the vision of John Bolton and the founding fathers became tangible reality. For it was during those twelve months that all the relevant sectors of the British establishment finally, unequivocally and irrevocably accepted management as a major thrust for education within universities' (p. 19). In the autumn of that year FME was prepared to launch the first of three major appeals.

From the 1960s other developments were taking place that provided additional impetus to the objectives of FME. In 1961, the Government established a National Economic Development Council. In its second report in 1963 it stated:

> There is a need for at least one very high-level new school or institute, somewhat on the lines of the Harvard Business School or the School of Industrial Management at MIT. This should help to provide better trained managers for industry, more trained teachers for the technical colleges and a much needed centre for research into problems of management and education. More immediately the development and coordination of the work already proceeding in the technical colleges, colleges of advanced technology and the universities, would help to meet the urgent problems of providing better and more widely used educational facilities for management (Rose, 1970).

In the same year the Robbins Report on Higher Education recommended (in addition to giving the Colleges of Advanced Technology university status) that two postgraduate schools for management education should be established to supplement other developments already taking place in a number of institutions.

Divergent views as to how to progress management education still existed among top industrialists. In an effort to resolve these, Lord Rootes invited key players to dinner on 17 July 1963. The outcome was to invite Lord Franks to review the situation and to make recommendations. Since he was an academic, a businessman and a diplomat, he was a credible choice for all parties. It took Franks only four months to make his report of 12 pages. Among the recommendations were two high-quality business schools should be established and that they should be part of a university but enjoying considerable autonomy as a partnership between the university and business; these schools should not slow down the existing growth of management education in other universities and technical colleges. The FBI put its full weight behind the planned appeal to enable the recommendations to be implemented. It should be noted that Sir Norman Kipping was the Director-General of the FBI during this time (1946–1965), and that his managerial experiences at Standard Telephone and Cables before and at the Ministry of Production during the War had made him a strong supporter of management education (Larson, 2009). Lord Normanbrook was invited to head the working party to prepare the appeal. By the end of 1964 industry had raised £5 million, and this was to be matched by Government.

In the light of the events developing in relation to the Franks Report, FME suspended its separate appeal that would enable it to meet its commitments to ongoing projects. The joint appeal launched in 1964 was sponsored by the FBI, the BIM and the FME. In addition to the main proposal of a business school in London and one in Manchester, provision was made that would enable FME commitments to be met at the universities of Durham, Edinburgh, Glasgow, Liverpool, London (LSE and Imperial) and Manchester, at institutions soon to be universities (Strathclyde and Aston) and at the Regent Street Polytechnic. A sum was also budgeted for the expansion of management education at other universities and colleges known to be preparing applications for funds to the UGC and to industry. The FBI and BIM (John Bolton was then chair of their Council) asked FME to administer the Fund according to agreed principles.

The first Principal of London Business School (LBS) was appointed in April 1965 — Dr Arthur Earle, a Canadian businessman. He was working in Britain as Managing Director of Hoover UK at the time of his appointment. The first intake into its postgraduate programme was made in October 1966. At Manchester Business School (MBS), Grigor McClelland (a businessman turned academic) was appointed Director in September 1965, and its first intake of students occurred in the same month. During the period 1962–1967, the UGC had to make special grants for the early management education initiatives in other universities, but in the next quinquennium it wanted management studies to be included in the block grants made to individual universities. But because of the funding problem facing the UGC at that time FME had to finance the costs of the schemes implemented in Bradford, Hull and Leeds for two years in order to maintain the momentum that had been generated. Funds were also made available for short courses and for research at Ashridge, Henley, Roffey Park (which had links with Sussex), Cranfield and Cambridge.

A problem which several had foreseen attracted attention in 1965/1966 — teacher training and development for management education. Several initiatives were made to help solve the problem. These were funded by the FME, the Department of Education and Science (DES) and the Ford

Foundation. They included sending individuals to courses in American business schools, and to inviting distinguished American professors to contribute to courses organized in the United Kingdom. The need for 300 new teachers was one of the main recommendations of the Rose Report (Rose, 1970). A special panel under the chairmanship of the FME Chairman was set up to investigate the supply of teachers. A major contributor to the supply was the International Teachers Programme which Harvard had brought across to Europe in 1970; a consortium of European business schools gradually took over the organizations of the programme. In 1972, FME financed a British Case Clearing House based at Cranfield School of Management so that teaching materials became less dependent on American sources. Other initiatives in the teaching area included: the availability of fellowships so that senior businessmen from production, finance, marketing or industrial relations could attend a business school for one year with the intention of taking up an academic career; financing a project proposed by Lancaster University's School of Management and Organisational Sciences for a Management Teacher Development Unit. Donald Binsted (Imperial Chemical Industries (ICI) organization development adviser) was the first director and John Burgoyne the research director. Renamed the Centre for the Study of Management Learning its success (including a part-time MA in Management Learning) was evidenced by being given departmental status in 1984.

In 1967, the Council of Industry for Management Education (CIME) was born. This was the result of a tripartite meeting of the CBI (formerly FBI), BIM and FME at which the CBI had expressed concern about the number of bodies now associated with management education, and no single body to express industry's perceived needs in the field. CIME was formed to fulfil this function, and included the Chairmen of BIM, FME and CBI's Education and Training Committee. One of the strengths of FME was the formidable networks to which its Council members belonged. These served as constructive links to other organizations as well as ensuring that divergent views benefited its deliberations. For example, Jim Platt and John Bolton served on the UGC's Business and Management Studies subcommittee; J. G. W. Davies (Bank of England) and John Marsh (BIM) were members of the National Economic Development Office (NEDO) Management Education and Development Committee; Platt chaired the UK Advisory Council on Education for Management, and Sir David Watherston the DMS committee; five members were Chairmen of Industrial Training Boards; others were on the governing bodies of Henley, Ashridge, Scottish Business School, LBS and MBS (Nind, 1985).

Access to additional networks was obtained as successive Directors of FME served on a number of committees, including: the UGC Business and Management Studies subcommittee, the Social Science Research Council (SSRC)/Economic and Social Research Council (ESRC), the Council for

National Academic Awards (CNAA) and the NEDO Management Education, Training and Development Committee. These various links enabled the FME to play a consistent part in the encouragement of a coherent national policy for management education. Indeed, apart from its role in the establishment of LBS and MBS, the FME provided pump-priming finance to help set up other initiatives which were subsequently supported by the UGC and the research councils. This policy enabled it to spread its influence across 37 universities/colleges and 12 Regional Management Centres (RMCs) (Nind, 1985). Its second appeal in 1970 enabled it to make substantial grants (apart from LBS and MBS) to the development of business schools in the Midlands and Yorkshire (i.e. Aston, Bradford and Warwick) and to Central Scotland (i.e. Edinburgh, Glasgow and Strathclyde). The appeal also resulted in substantial grants being made to the three independent colleges of Henley, Ashridge and Roffey Park.

A problem that surfaced in the 1960s was the anxiety surrounding the postgraduate award of the DMS which had been inaugurated in 1961. Many felt that it did not carry the status it was intended to carry in industry and commerce. The Platt Report (1968) reviewed the situation and made recommendations, many of which were subsequently implemented including the establishment of the RMCs in the 1970s. A government-led initiative created 12 of these centres, each consisting of groups of polytechnics and technical colleges. They were created over a number of years, and were partly financed by local authorities. Initially their main focus was the DMS mentioned earlier, but they soon introduced a BSc in Business Studies which was accredited by the CNAA. These centres were also supported by grants from FME. Prior to awarding a grant constructive visits were made by panels with representatives of the CBI, BIM and FME.

The American Association of Colleges and Schools of Business (AACSB) was the established body for accrediting American business schools. In the late 1960s and early 1970s FME initiated several exchanges of information with them in order to gauge the desirability of a similar single body emerging in the United Kingdom. Although this idea was premature for the UK business school sector at this time, two related developments did take place and were financially supported by FME in their formative years: in 1972 the Conference (later Council) of University Management Schools (CUMS), and in 1973 the Association of Regional Management Centres (ARMC) were formed. ARMC later merged with another body to form the Association of Management Education Centres (AMEC). In 1987, AMEC merged with the Standing Committee on Business Schools to form the Association of Management and Business Education (AMBE) to represent the polytechnics and higher education college providers. As we shall see later, CUMS and AMBE merged to form the ABS in 1992.

The valuable networking role of the FME has already been referred to above. Other initiatives should be mentioned that acted to keep business and management education to the fore, and to stimulate further positive developments. One of these was the establishment of a fellowship in 1977 at the Oxford Centre for Management Studies. The person appointed was an American journalist working in Britain, Nancy Foy. Her brief was to 'review management education, its problems and needs, over the coming decade, and to suggest areas where initiatives could be taken' (Nind, 1985, p. 68). Her report drew attention to the need for links between academic institutions and industry, and between academic institutions themselves. Industry wanted academic work to be more relevant to industry's needs; and academia wanted industry to be more ready to open its doors in the interest of joint research and learning (Foy, 1978). The Foy Report confirmed the value of FME in bringing together interested parties through conferences and seminars. This reinforced FME's activities in this area. The following was a typical example: a seminar at LBS in 1982 on leadership in management led by John Adair (from Surrey University) and involving Sir John Harvey-Jones (Chairman of ICI) and other senior industrialists.

FME was also instrumental in enabling the Open University to enter the management field with a distance learning course based on BIM's Effective Manager Programme. The Open University course 'The Effective Manager' was launched in 1983 and proved to be highly successful.

As already indicated the Council of FME consisted mainly of international businessmen, and therefore it is no surprise to read that in 1971 John Bolton wrote 'that management education transcends national boundaries and that the growth of an international spirit and international expertise should be promoted and encouraged wherever possible in the interest of British industry and the national economy' (Foy, 1978, p. 74). Although FME's constitution did not allow it to fund projects abroad, it was able to fund some British students to attend INSEAD as well as the international programme of the Ecole des Affaires de Paris (EAP). Both were very international in orientation and, in the case of EAP, students spent an equal amount of time in Paris, Oxford and Berlin. FME was also involved in European bodies; it was a member of the International University Contact for Management Education in 1969. This body merged with another European organization in 1971 (the European Association of Management Training Centres) to form the European Foundation for Management Development (EFMD) in Brussels; FME was a member of its Board of Trustees in the years 1977–1983. As we shall see later, EFMD has developed into a European institution that counterbalances the strong American influence on management education.

In recent years FME has continued to support British management education. The background to FME's current focus has been explained by the current director Mike Jones as:

> In 2002 we funded research undertaken by Lancaster into the supply and demand for Business School faculty as we were increasingly concerned by the constant increase in student numbers across the sector against the many retirements and demographic negatives that we were observing. That report made for disappointing reading in as much as it came up with a figure that to keep pace the sector needed to recruit 400 new academics per year for at least 5 years. We do not recruit even 100 a year and these that are recruited are either off Post doc Fellowships or from overseas, neither of whom are much use in the post grad teaching world. The demands of the RAE upon institutions has made it almost impossible for those without a PhD to move into academia and so in our own small way we have been trying to do something about the situation (personal communication, 10 March 2010).

Its concern over this situation, and for 'relevance' in management education, has meant that over the past seven years FME has focused on increasing numbers on its fellowship scheme. Currently there are 26 fellows at various business schools, enabling 'the mid-career business practitioner move into a second career as a business school academic'.

1.6.   Corporate-Based Business and Management Education

In the latter half of the twentieth century, major corporations and professional bodies associated with the functional areas of management, had come to accept the value of management education. However, some felt that their organization had more to gain if they could exert more control over the content of courses and the learning processes involved. Hence, this led to the development of in-house and tailor-made external courses, and the recently formed corporate universities. Management consultancy firms recognized the growing need for the education and training of both functional managers (e.g. marketing) and general managers, and began to market appropriate courses. The larger ones created residential centres that competed with the independent management colleges of Henley, Ashridge and Roffey Park in their early days. Sundridge Park, for instance, was part of PA Consulting Group. The mansion that formed the centre functioned as a luxury hotel after the Second World War, and became a management centre in 1956. Large companies also began to establish their own management centres; e.g. NatWest at Heythrop Park.

Both the company-based centres and the independent colleges were initially concerned with management development and training. However, the colleges soon broadened out to running degrees in management. Thus, Henley was able to do this in conjunction with Brunel University, Ashridge with City University, and Roffey Park with Sussex University. In 1997 Henley was able to award its own degrees, and similarly Ashridge in 2008.

Several business schools have catered for the market of tailor-made programmes for corporations. These were sometimes designed to meet the education/training needs of single organizations, and sometimes for consortia of organizations. Often they enabled managers who satisfied the necessary criteria to be awarded MScs/MBAs. Early models for these programmes in the late 1980s and 1990s were run by Cass, Warwick and Lancaster business schools for companies such as Sainsbury, Coopers and Lybrand, and British Airways, respectively. The experiences of Lancaster with the latter formed the basis of a conference paper (Davies & Kelly, 1994). It is clear that the diverse cultures of two service organizations create problems that require an experimental period before they are resolved. Moreover, the contractual relationships of such partnership programmes tend to limit their lifespan for any client organization.

A corporate university is another development imported from the United States. The model of McDonald's Hamburger University has not as yet generated much enthusiasm in the United Kingdom, since it is more of a training institution and misappropriates the title of 'university'.

1.7. Observations on the Milestones in the Development of Business and Management Education

This overview has covered a wide range of individuals, reports and institutions. The content would have been much greater if the historical analysis had been as thorough as Edward Brech's monumental 5-volume work 'The Evolution of Modern Management in Britain 1832–1979' (Brech, 2002); or if the equivalent American features to influence thinking in the United Kingdom had been included. Box 1.2 tries to bring together the UK features in a chronological sequence so as to underline the historical perspective, and to serve as an anchor for the reader trying to place events in some sort of order. Key reports, as opposed to institutions, are in italics. Some items are yet to be mentioned in later sections.

Box 1.2.   Milestones in the development of business and management education in the United Kingdom.

1754	Society for the Encouragement of Arts, Manufactures and Commerce.
1847	Institution of Mechanical Engineers (IME).
1901–1903	Early academic intervention by LSE, Manchester, and Birmingham.
1913	Welfare Workers' Association (now Chartered Institute of Personnel and Development)
1919	Institute of Cost and Works Accountants.
1919	Association for the Advancement of Education in Industry and Commerce (AEIC).
1919	British Association for Commercial Education (in 1934 BACIE now part of IPD).
1920	Institute of Industrial Administration (IIA) (now Chartered Management Institute).
1922	National Institute of Industrial Psychology (NIIP).
1925	Regent Street Polytechnic course for IMEs on Workshop Organisation and Management.
1926	Management Research Groups (MRG).
1934	Pioneering consultancies 'Production Engineering Ltd' and 'Urwick Orr Partnership'.
1937	British Management Council (subsequently replaced by BIM).
1945	*Baillieu Report (proposes formation of BIM).*
1945	*Percy Report, 'Higher Technological Education'.*
1947	*Urwick Report, 'Education for Management' (proposes Diploma in Management).*
1947	Administrative Staff College at Henley.
1948	British Institute of Management (BIM).
1952	British Productivity Council.
1956	Sundridge Park Management Centre (part of PA Consultants).
1957	Merger of BIM and IIA completed.
1959	Ashridge Management College.
1960	Association of Teachers of Management (ATM) (later Association of Management Education and Development or AMED).
1960	Foundation for Management Education.

1961	*National Economic Development Council (mission to improve competitive power; their 1963 report identifies the need for management education and research).*
1963	*Robbins Report, 'Higher Education'.*
1963	*Franks Report (recommends two major business schools).*
1964	*Crick Report (recommendations compatible with Robbins re undergraduates).*
1964	Council for National Academic Awards (CNAA) (approves qualifications in non-university institutions).
1965	Central Training Council.
1965	Oxford Centre for Management Studies.
1965	Confederation of British Industry (CBI) (emerges from three older employer bodies: Federation of British Industries, British Employers' Confederation, National Association of British Manufacturers).
1965	*NEDO 'Management, Recruitment* & Development'.
1965	Manchester Business School (MBS) (year of first MBA/MSc intake).
1966	London Business School (LBS) (year of first MBA/MSc intake).
1966	Onwards business schools founded in former CATs, 'new' and 'old' universities.
1967	Council of Industry for Management Education (CIME) (created by CBI, BIM, and FME so as to have single body to express Industry's needs re Management education).
1967	Graduate Business Association formed (forerunner of Association of MBAs; AMBA).
1968	*Fulton Report (Civil Service College recommended).*
1970	*Rose Report (highlights need for future management teachers).*
1970	*Mant, 'The Experienced Manager' (Questions raised as to who are the consumers for management education).*
1971	*Owen Report (Critical of the output of business schools and quality of teachers).*
1971	Council of University Management Schools (CUMS).
1972	Roffey Park Management Centre (established in 1946 but involved in management education from 1972).
1973	Association of Regional Management Centres (ARMC).
1985	Jarratt Report (response to the need for universities to become more efficient and accountable for public funds).
1986	British Academy of Management (the learned body in the United Kingdom representing management education and research).

1986	Council for Industry and Higher Education (CIHE) established.
1987	Association of Management and Business Education (AMBE).
1987	*Handy et al., 'The Making of Managers'.*
1987	*Constable/McCormick Report.*
1988	National Forum for Management Education and Development (established with government and big firm support; Management Charter Initiative (MCI) its main operational arm).
1992	Further and Higher Education Act (64 polytechnics and some higher education colleges gain university status).
1992	HEFCE introduces first Research Assessment Exercise (RAE) (method for distributing research money based on the quality of an institution's research).
1992	Association of Business Schools (ABS) (formed when CUMS and AMBE merge).
1994	*Bain Report (Commission on Management Research).*
1996	European Quality Link (EQUAL) (created to promote continuous improvement in quality of management education in Europe; support group for EQUIS — European Quality Improvement Scheme).
2002	*Cleaver Report 'Raising our Game' (Council for Excellence in Management and Leadership; CEML).*
2002	Advanced Institute of Management Research (AIM) created.
2003	*Lambert Review of Business-University Collaboration.*
2006	*UK National Forum for Employers and Business School Deans Report.*

Reviewing this chapter, a number of observations come to mind: the 'randomness' in the early development of management education in the United Kingdom; the virtual invisibility of academia in this early development; most of the early 'leadership' is provided by industrialists and professional associations; the two World Wars stimulated activity relevant to management education (e.g. National Institute of Industrial Psychology (NIIP), consultancy, government-sponsored reports); 1960s characterized by events that propelled the development of formal management education and the emergence of a 'business school industry'. It is this latter feature that is the focus of Chapter 2.

Chapter 2

Bodies Representing and Regulating UK Business Schools

Management education in the United Kingdom took off in the early 1960s. As it expanded in universities and colleges it became clear to the leaders in the field that there was much to be gained through co-operation as well as competition. Educational institutions competed with one another for people (students and staff) and finance (both private and public). This meant that they had to develop quality products and services to survive in a demanding market environment. The benefits of co-operation included enhancing opportunities for exchanging learning experiences and, by the development of powerful pressure groups, for influencing decisions and events in the environment. This chapter is concerned with the bodies that emerged to facilitate learning and survival, and to enhance the quality and influence of business schools.

2.1. Council for National Academic Awards

While this section is primarily concerned with 'business schools', it is necessary to cover the historical role of the CNAA in management education, particularly at the undergraduate level. The Crick Report is relevant in providing some of the background details, as the following paragraphs illustrate.

> On 24th July, 1961, the Minister of Education announced in Parliament that a Higher National Diploma in Business Studies was to be established as an award to be obtained by way of either a two year's full-time or a three year's sandwich course. He went on the say that the National Advisory Council on Education for Industry and Commerce had undertaken to consider the desirability of setting up a further

higher award in business studies in respect of courses broadly equivalent in length and standard to those leading to the Diploma in Technology. Following this announcement, we were appointed by the National Advisory Council in September 1961 to examine the nature and extent of the likely demand for the proposed further higher award in business studies, and the form which courses leading to such an award might take (Crick, 1964, p. 1).

In the light of discussions in other sections it is worth noting that Crick's committee included Douglas Hague (Professor of Applied Economics, Manchester University) and Tom Lupton (Head of the Department of Industrial Administration, Birmingham College of Advanced Technology). The committee delayed the publication of its report until it could take into account the Robbins Report on Higher Education (Robbins, 1963). It noted that the Diploma in Technology (Dip. Tech.) was to be replaced by degrees offered by the colleges of advanced technology (as the new technological universities), or by the proposed CNAA. The three main conclusions of the committee were first, there is a need for a new nationally recognized qualification in business studies comparable to the present Dip. Tech. (generally recognized as equivalent to honours degree standard and suitable for entry to postgraduate degrees); secondly, there is a demand from industry and commerce for people with such a qualification (particularly when organized on a sandwich basis); thirdly, this demand should increase as the value of the courses become apparent.

Before the introduction of the bachelors degrees in business studies under the supervisory control of the CNAA, the National Council for Technological Awards administered the Dip. Tech. qualification. 'At the end of March 1963, there were 111 Dip. Tech. courses in 16 subjects at 28 colleges; they were being followed by 7,310 students, including 2,715 first-year students'. The following extracts give one some idea of why 'business studies' should be included as an undergraduate degree in future developments:

> When we turn to 'business studies' we seek in vain for a crisp, accurate and comprehensive definition. Broadly, the term may be taken to encompass all those branches of study directed toward careers in business which are not of a technical kind (in the sense in which the word 'technical' is ordinarily understood. ... In our present context 'business' embraces buying and selling at all stages and the holding, handling and distribution of goods, the service trades and many ancillary activities such as banking, insurance and investment. ... In our understanding the basic disciplines appropriate to business

studies are economics, sociology and mathematics. .... But in studying and using these disciplines the student must be helped to develop qualities of imagination and enterprise, and powers of understanding, criticism and judgment, if he is to be successful in a business career.

We have not included in this definition any reference to management or management studies, though it is clear that some exercise of managerial or administrative functions is involved in nearly all responsible positions in business. We recognize that the content of the courses we propose may in many respects be similar to that of some branches of management education; but we are here concerned with undergraduate work, and it is now customary to apply the term 'management studies' only to postgraduate courses. Nevertheless, the business studies courses we propose should equip students, after responsible experience, the better to perform managerial functions, and might well form the foundation for management studies. To this extent, as in the type of course we recommend, our proposals seem to fit the need which the National Economic Development Council has underlined for larger national investment in business and management studies (Crick, 1964).

The report goes on to argue for the need for a qualification that is at a higher level than the recently introduced Higher National Certificate/Diploma in business studies in various colleges; particularly in the light of the very limited university courses with a bias towards business. Among the evidences quoted was the result of a survey of members of the FBI which showed that the Higher National Diploma in business studies had not removed the need for a more advanced award. As to the form and content of such an award, the report stresses the need to link academic study with practical experience; thus the preference for the 'sandwich' format. The basic disciplines relevant to business should provide the grounding for the award. In order for an honours degree standard to be attached to the award, and for local firms to support the award, the recommendation is for well-resourced colleges to be selected and for the learning content to reflect the predominant local business activities. The report welcomed the proposal of Robbins Committee that the CNAA should replace the National Council for Technological Awards. The 'new Council would be empowered to grant degrees in areas of study outside science and technology, including business studies, and it therefore seems clear to us that the establishment and administration of the new award should fall within the Council's functions'.

The interest of relevant professional bodies in the proposed award is recognized, and it was hoped that an honours equivalent degree would encourage the main professional bodies to give exemption of its holders to some of their professional examination requirements.

When the DMS qualification was launched in 1961 it was administered by the DES. In 1976 it was placed under the authority of the CNAA, and 'by the late 1980s it was established as the largest general management programme in the UK with some 7,700 managers enrolled. The DMS was taught almost exclusively in the Polytechnics and Colleges of Higher Education. Its principal success lay in the preparation for managerial responsibilities of people who were emerging from predominantly technical roles. The course was also well supported by public sector industries as a recognized training route. It was estimated in a report to CNAA in 1990 that close to 90% of the managers attending DMS courses were supported by their employers' (Miles, 1996, p. 4).

When the CNAA ceased operation in 1992 it had become the largest degree-awarding body in the United Kingdom. 'More than a third of all students who are studying for a degree in this country attend CNAA-approved courses. ... CNAA ensures that its awards are comparable to those of universities, professional associations and employers. When considering the academic merits of courses. ... It also takes account of the college environment and the quality of the total educational experience offered' (CNAA, 1989–1990). It was accrediting undergraduate business studies degrees in 47 polytechnics/colleges (e.g. Birmingham Polytechnic, Manchester Polytechnic, Newcastle upon Tyne Polytechnic, Anglia Higher Education College, West Glamorgan Institute of Higher Education). Further discussion relating to the CNAA will be found in other sections, particularly in Chapter 4 (i.e. Case studies: Undergraduate Management Education).

2.2.   CUMS, AMBE and ABS

The short history of the ABS has already been published (Williams, 2007). It is an important body for UK business schools, and a summary of its history is relevant. When ABS came into existence in 1992 it was the result of a merger between bodies that went back over 20 years — CUMS and AMBE. In 1970 an informal network of deans/directors of university-based business and management schools began to take shape. Several forces brought this about. First, there was the rapid expansion of management schools as a result of the Robbins Report, the creation of the FME and the Franks Report. Secondly, given the investment of major corporations in the new business schools (via the FME) they began to question the early returns from business schools (e.g. Owen, 1970). Thirdly, the majority of teachers involved in the masters programmes were learning to transfer knowledge and skills to a new audience (i.e. budding managers instead of economists, psychologists, accountants etc.). Fourthly, many schools based in universities encountered problems as colleagues questioned their academic credibility, and found themselves facing new competition for limited university resources. It was against this background that Professors Kempner of Henley, Beresford-Dew of UMIST and Moore of LBS initiated the CUMS in 1971.

At that time CUMS was intended to be an informal forum for discussing current issues and disseminating information relevant to business schools. The 12 schools represented at the first meeting agreed to elect a Chair annually; a more formal structure was only introduced when membership reached 27. CUMS was instrumental in negotiating a loan scheme with Midland Bank in 1973 to assist postgraduates in management education; it also developed links with other bodies that subsequently proved useful. These bodies included: the European Foundation for Management Education, Department of Education and Science, Graduate Business Association (forerunner of AMBA) and the Association of Regional Management Centres. Several joint activities were arranged with the latter body in the 1970s, e.g. management teacher development, annual conferences.

In 1977, CUMS became less of a talking shop (with a traditional annual dinner at Henley) and more of a pressure group. By the late 1980s it had become an effective agent for its member business schools and for management education in general. A good example of this was under the Chairmanship of Professor Andrew Thomson (Open University). Professors Griffiths and Murray (City University Business School) published a paper in 1985 promoting the proposition that business schools in the United Kingdom should be privatized (Griffiths & Murray, 1985). The anxiety of the business school community (and the universities) was aroused when the then Minister of Education, Sir Keith Joseph, declared his sympathy for this proposal. One of the consequences was a meeting initiated by Bob Horton, Chairman of BP and of the CIME. At this meeting senior representatives from five key stakeholders in business and management education were present: Bob Horton representing CIME, John Stoddart of the CNAA representing the polytechnic sector, John Constable the Director of the Institute of Management, Andrew Thomson of CUMS and Sir David Hancock the Permanent Secretary at the DES.

The main outcome of the meeting was the setting up of working parties, and their efforts were brought together in the influential report of Constable and McCormick (1987). Bob Horton seconded McCormick to co-ordinate the project and also provided an office in BP. Following this pathway was a neat way of shelving the privatization proposal, but the whole episode had favourable consequences for business schools. Business schools became much more aware of a common problem they shared, i.e. the tendency of being treated as 'cash cows' by their universities. The authoritative findings also helped in the development of the sector in other ways: it recognized that effective management was a key factor in economic growth; Britain's managers lacked the education and development opportunities of their competitors; anticipated growth would highlight major deficiencies in the supply of management education and development; management schools should remain in their parent academic institutions but should have greater managerial and financial autonomy.

Under the Chairmanship of Professor (now Sir) George Bain, CUMS geared itself to taking a more active role to promote and defend the business school sector. In 1988/1989 it became a company limited by guarantee and a charity, and employed its own part-time administrator. Direct representations were made to government re the Handy Report in 1987, and the Constable/McCormick Report in the same year; in 1988, representations were made to the UGC re the Research Selectivity Exercise (RSE), and individuals were briefed in the House of Lords before the debate on management education. The attention of various government departments and agencies (e.g. ESRC) was drawn to the lack of representation of the business schools on their committees, using both formal submissions and informal interactions to achieve results. All these activities bore fruit in that some well-known names in business schools found themselves on targeted committees. They included: George Bain, John Constable, Leo Murray, Andrew Thomson, Andrew Pettigrew, Stephen Watson and John Burgoyne.

It was mentioned above that CUMS developed some joint activities with the AMECs in the 1970s. This body, together with others, came together to form the AMBE in 1987. AMBE now represented 85 major business and management units in polytechnics and colleges, and aspired to form a single authoritative body that could be seen to represent all the providers of business and management education in the 'public' sector (i.e. the non-university sector partly controlled by the local authorities). Although CUMS and AMBE had evolved independently of each other, a number of factors brought them closer together in the late 1980s and early 1990s. These included: the 1992 Higher Education Act which abolished the 'binary line' dividing the polytechnics and the university sectors; the demise of the CNAA; collaboration between the two bodies had already taken place; and they complemented each other — CUMS focusing primarily on postgraduate and executive management education and on research, and AMBE on broader business studies at the undergraduate level and a hierarchy of post-experience and postgraduate management programmes. It was therefore little surprising when CUMS and AMBE set up a working party to explore the feasibility of creating a joint body representing all major providers of business and management education in the higher education sector. Protracted negotiations and effective leadership on the part of various stakeholders resulted in the formation of a merged body in 1992 — the ABS and Jonathan Slack was appointed as Chief Officer.

The objects for which ABS was established were spelt out in the Memorandum and Articles of Association dated 22 September 1992; these are reproduced in Box 2.1.

This broad remit of ABS reflected its potential for advancing management education, and in continuing some of the responsibilities of the CNAA (initial office space and administrative help were provided by this body). ABS was a structure to enable national consistency among well-established programmes such as the BA (Hons) Business Studies, the DMS and the MBA; and it facilitated collective discussion of recent innovations such as Credit Accumulation Transfer Scheme (CATS), Accreditation Prior Learning (APL), competence-based management standards and the National Council for Vocational Qualifications (NCVQs). These collective discussions led to one of ABS' early initiatives — the formation of a national consortium for the verification of awards. The MVC was formed as a subsidiary of ABS towards the end of 1992, and provided a robust verification process by which individual business and management schools might award MCI endorsed

---

Box 2.1. Memorandum and articles of association of ABS.

'To advance the education of the public in business and management in particular through the promotion of business and management education training and development so as to improve the quality and effectiveness of the practice of management in the United Kingdom. In furtherance of such objects but not otherwise the company may:

- Promote effective forms of organization administration teaching and research within institutions delivering undergraduate, postgraduate or post-experience business and management education.
- Promote research organizational structures and communications between members and the public and government to assist its members in their contributions to society at large.
- Provide a forum for the exchange of ideas and stimulate discussion on the role of business and management education.
- Organise and facilitate the development of the competence of all academic and administrative staff of member organizations.
- Carry out any other role in the nature of assistance promotion investigation and exchange of information about business management education training and development generally.'

NVQs and Scottish Vocational Qualifications (SVQ) in management and other areas. Both ABS and the Institute of Management appointed representative directors on the MVC board. By 1999, ABS re-evaluated its relationship with MVC. There were several reasons for this: MVC needed more resources to retain approval of MCI; a close working relationship had developed with the Institute of Management; changes in government funding and lack of employer support led to a decline in the demand for these qualifications (i.e. NVQs and SVQs); concern had developed that the NCVQ framework was too close to a re-emergence of the CNAA. Accordingly, ABS decided to transfer ownership of Management Verification Qualifications (MVQ) to the Institute of Management.

As an aside it is worth pointing out that the MCI was an outcome of an accumulation of factors in the late 1980s and early 1990s that highlighted the lack of professional expertise and qualifications among British managers relative to overseas competition: the findings of a CNAA working party under the Chairmanship of Sir Ron Dearing; the Constable/McCormick Report (Constable & McCormick, 1987); the Handy Report (Handy, Gordon, et al., 1987); and the Cannon and Taylor Report (Cannon & Taylor, 1994). The first part of the latter report summarized the results of a working party chaired by Tom Cannon which attempted to identify changes and progress made between 1987 and 1994 following the Constable/ McCormick Report and Handy Report. Their conclusions included the following observations: the numbers studying for undergraduate business studies degrees significantly exceeded the targets for 1995; there had been a sharp increase in MBAs and equivalent degrees in the late 1980s; the post-1992 universities provided three times as many places at undergraduate level, but the older universities were the main providers of full-time MBAs; the National Forum for Management Education and Development (established in 1988 with the support of government and several big firms) aimed at acting as a catalyst for change by focusing on management development, but its main operational and marketing vehicle (MCI) had mixed results. The limited impact of MCI was reflected in the poor take-up among the older universities. As Burgoyne pointed out, 'In functions dealing with high levels of uncertainty, there is little of use in the competence framework which is past focused' (1988). The MCI's competency-based approach has also been criticized for undervaluing knowledge and theory, and for ignoring the international dimension of management education.

Nevertheless accreditation of programmes and schools remained a concern of ABS, as they had been for the earlier constituent bodies of CUMS and AMBE. These concerns were also felt by another national body, Association of MBAs or AMBA, and by the international EFMD. Since 1919 the United States had successfully operated an accreditation body for their business schools —AACSB.

Box 2.2.   ABS membership criteria.

Membership is available to Institutions which are universities, colleges, schools or any other bodies which satisfy all of the following criteria:

- Delivery in the United Kingdom of higher education level qualifications in the business and administrative studies area as defined by Higher Education Statistics Agency (HESA).
- Have gained formal approval from the Privy Council and either approval by the QAA or Qualifications and Curriculum Agency (QCA)/Scottish Qualifications Authority (SQA) for their qualifications.
- Demonstrable commitment to research or scholarship in relation to their qualifications.

In considering the third criteria and whether an institution can demonstrate a commitment to research or scholarship, the following will be taken into account:

the Institutional strategy and policies,
the quality and quantity of published outputs and
the existence of and support for the 'community of scholars' associated with the qualifications.

Institutions applying for membership should provide evidence and detailed information on all of the above and may be required to facilitate a visit by one or more members of the Executive prior to approval. The cost of such a visit is borne by the applying Institution.

Appendix 2 is a current list of bodies that are members of ABS. Certain criteria have to be satisfied to qualify for membership. These are listed in Box 2.2, and are presented as approved by members at the Annual General Meeting in 2008. Some institutions may be given Associate Status at the discretion of the ABS Executive, and as such they do not have voting rights. This enables UK institutions that as yet do not meet criteria for membership, or overseas institutions, accrediting organizations and corporate providers that have an interest in management education, to maintain a mutually beneficial relationship with ABS.

2.3.   Association of MBAs

The nearest to AACSB in the United Kingdom was the service provided by AMBA. As their initial label conveyed (i.e. Business Graduates Association)

AMBA was an association of individuals who qualified at 'recognized' business schools. When it was established in June 1967 it had few members (eight US MBAs and two LBS MBAs). By 1985 MBAs from 26 UK providers could become members. By 1990 providers grew to 76 and 'quality' had become an issue. In the intervening years AMBA ceased to accept members from new schools, and developed their first accreditation criteria against which to assess the quality of MBA programmes. By 1987 the stakeholder group had expanded from graduate members to accredited business schools and MBA employers. Today AMBA offers a well-developed international accreditation service which has been drawn upon by 158 business schools in 72 countries. It accredits Doctor of Business Administration (DBA) and pre-experience Masters programmes as well as MBAs, and has a membership network of some 9000. Its vision as expressed on the Internet:

> Our vision is to be recognised internationally as the author-itative voice in postgraduate management education. The achievement of our vision depends on four strategic objectives which will bring together our key stakeholders: business schools, MBA students and alumni and employers. Specifically we will:
>
> • Continue to deliver a world class accreditation service focusing on the quality assurance of postgraduate general management programmes at the top tier business schools.
> • Strengthen our collaborative relationships with our accre-dited business schools, providing them with relevant insights, intelligence and networks to give them the advantage in a competitive environment.
> • Support our exclusive global network of MBA students and graduates and deliver services that will assist them in their professional development and lifelong learning.
> • Engage with business and MBA employers, building awareness of the Association's reputation, the benefits of accreditation and our professional network.

2.4.   European Foundation for Management Education

Since the development of quality education in business and management was one of the main aims of ABS, it was natural for it to become actively involved in the accreditation industry. In the mid-1990s ABS recognized that it made sense that there should be a single accreditation body in the United Kingdom. A joint ABS/AMBA working party was formed to define the relevant criteria for accreditation. The working party's output was in terms of two levels of accreditation — a threshold and an excellence level. In 1997, a ballot of ABS members on whether they should establish an MBA accreditation process showed an overwhelming 89% in favour of a UK-wide scheme. However, AMBA was concerned about the level of abstentions from six of its accredited schools. Negotiations stalled when AMBA declared that they would be setting up their own scheme based on the 'excellence' level of the working party. However, the experience gained by ABS efforts was put to good effect in two further ways. First it produced, at the request of the Quality Assurance Agency (QAA), benchmarking statements for business and management education programmes. Secondly, it took a leading role in the formation of EQUAL (Equal Quality Link). This latter development had been brought about by the AACSB 'threat' of spreading its accreditation tentacles to Europe. Both AMBA and AACSB tried to persuade EFMD to accept them as the accrediting bodies, but EFMD accepted that ABS was the authentic representative of UK business schools and together with AMBA, Asociacion Espanola de Representantes de Escuelas de Direction de Empresa (AAEDE) (Spain), Associazione per la Formazione alla Direzione Aziendale (ASFOR) (Italy), Le Chapitre (France) and EFMD, EQUAL was duly established in June 1996 as an independent association. Its objectives included:

- Creating an open forum for the exchange of information, benchmarking and co-operation between members in order to promote continuous improvement of quality in management education across Europe.
- Improving the quality of the processes through which institutions and programmes are assessed.
- Acting as the support group for a European accreditation system — the EQUIS.
- Furthering the internationalization of European management education, particularly by defining the criteria by which institutions can be assessed as having reached an international standing in their operations.

The formation of ABS, AMBA and EFMD has undoubtedly contributed to the development of the business schools industry in the United Kingdom, and with AACSB, to an industry worldwide. AACSB is the oldest established accrediting body having been founded in 1916 with the goal of enhancing the quality of management education in the United States. In 1995 it began to extend its accreditation programme internationally, and by 2006 it accredited 85 business schools outside the United States, including 35 in Europe (Trapnell, 2007). EFMD's EQUIS, and AMBA started accrediting business schools outside their domestic frontiers at roughly the same time. An important difference between the accreditation of EQUIS and AMBA was that the former assessed a school as a whole (including its mission and strategies, similar to AACSB), whereas the latter focused more on specific programmes (e.g. MBAs, similar in effect to professional bodies) (Greensted, 2000). The AACSB framework inevitably reflected the American culture, having been developed for internal use over some 80 years. In contrast the EQUIS framework reflected an appreciation for diversity, being devised by an international group, and emphasized the international dimension of management education from the outset (Urgel, 2007).

Chapter 3

The Growth of Knowledge-based Management Education

The evolution of modern management in the United Kingdom has been well documented by others (Child, 1969; Brech, 2002; Wilson & Thomson, 2006). The industrial revolutions of the eighteenth and nineteenth centuries saw the emergence of an important new occupational group — 'the engineer'. The gradual disappearance of the owner families, and the large and complex forms of organizations characterizing the twentieth century, encouraged the emergence of several occupational groups linked to 'the manager'. During the past century these groups became more differentiated from each other with the formation of professional bodies. Thus, we have specialists in marketing, operations, human resource management, finance and accounting. These specialists usually report to senior managers who oversee the whole business and are responsible for guiding organizational mission and strategies. This simplified picture will enable us to explore the main purpose of this chapter, which is to draw attention to some of the main thought leaders, and research programmes, contributing to the knowledge disseminated by professional bodies and business schools.

The development of business and management education as we know it today has depended upon the growth of relevant knowledge. The assumption being made by educators is that there is a body of knowledge which, if acquired by individuals in managerial roles, will render them more effective in these roles. Three questions arise from this assumption: What does this body of knowledge consist of? How was the quality of this body of knowledge monitored and improved? What learning processes facilitate the acquisition of this knowledge?

3.1. The Content of Business and Management Knowledge

Beliefs related to management effectiveness have always existed since the days when individuals found themselves operating within organized groups for the purpose of achieving given objectives. The fact that 'managers' as an occupational group were not written about can be explained in terms of cultural factors. In early societies this knowledge was passed on through social interactions and the writings of religious leaders, philosophers and others. It is not the purpose of this publication to explore these ancient historical roots, but to focus on the thinkers and researchers who have had a visible impact on the body of knowledge that has been disseminated through the educational initiatives identified in the 'milestones' in Box 1.2.

As we saw in Chapter 1 a number of institutions emerged from the eighteenth century and later which were concerned with the professional standing of their members, and in the sharing and advancement of knowledge underlying their activities. An early example was the Institution of Mechanical Engineers. The Society for the Encouragement of Arts, Manufactures and Commerce was an example of a body interested in furthering the wider technological and commercial achievements of the United Kingdom. As of today, available knowledge was disseminated through publications (books and journals), lectures, formal courses as well as informal social interaction.

Census returns of the number of managers have only been available since 1911 — the 629,000 in that Census had grown to 4,676,000 in the 2001 Census (Wilson & Thomson, 2006). These figures camouflage the difficulty of defining a 'manager', but there can be no doubt that the knowledge and skills of such a large disparate occupational group have had a significant impact on the UK economy. Practitioners and academics, who are able to share their knowledge, are a valuable human resource. Frederick Taylor's *Principles of Scientific Management* is a good example of how a set of principles formulated by an author can affect thinking and practice over many years, not only in his own native the United States but equally in the United Kingdom (Taylor, 1911). This book was an expanded version of an earlier publication that brought together lessons he had learnt as an engineer in a steel works (Taylor, 1903). For Taylor the principle object of management was to maximize the prosperity of both employer and employee. This meant sustained profitability for the employer, high wages and opportunity to reach maximum performance for the employee. He was accordingly puzzled by the inefficiency present in the workplace, given the 'common interest' of both groups. He suggested three causes for this state of affairs (Pugh & Hickson, 2007):

> First, the fallacious belief of the workers that any increase in output would inevitably result in unemployment; second, the defective systems of management which make it necessary for workers to restrict output in order to protect their interests; third, inefficient rule-of-thumb, effort-wasting methods of work.

This diagnosis led Taylor to put forward four principles of management: the development of a true science of work (involving scientific investigations to establish what a worker should achieve under given conditions, and rewarded by high rates of pay); the scientific selection and progressive development of the worker (once it was established that they had the abilities to achieve high output they should be trained to use the best methods); bringing together these two principles by management (he saw management as being the main resister to the adoption of scientific management); the constant and intimate co-operation of management and workers (both groups are subject to the same guidance provided by the scientific study of work, and both perform the tasks that they are best fitted to doing — management responsibilities being continuous supervision and control of the workers). The most visible legacy of Taylor's influence is in the development and application of 'Work Study' in the consultancy activities of such individuals as Frank and Lillian Gilbreth and Charles Bedaux. The underlying beliefs of his approach to management were maintained well after the Second World War.

Within the context of current knowledge scientific management can be criticized on the basis of the assumptions the approach is making about human behaviour and social institutions. However, it did bring to the fore the need to apply the general scientific approach to the study of issues of concern to management. Extracts from Taylor's 1911 publication (which was an expanded version of his 1903 book and the paper he gave to the American Society of Mechanical Engineers) expresses this aspect of his contribution in his own words:

> We can see our forests vanishing ... our soil carried by floods into the sea. ... But our wastes of human effort, which go on every day through such of our acts as are blundering, ill-directed, or inefficient ... are less visible, less tangible, and are but vaguely appreciated. ... Their appreciation calls for an act of memory, an effort of the imagination. ... This paper has been written: First, to point out ... the great loss which the whole country is suffering through inefficiency. ... Second, to try to convince the reader that the remedy ... lies in systematic management, rather than in searching for some unusual or extraordinary man. ... Third, to prove that the best manage-ment is in true science, resting upon clearly defined laws, rules, and principles, as a foundation ... (p. 5 & p. 7).

Consultation of various scholarly works will show that a number of other authors were also influential in developing what may be classified as the 'classical perspective' of management thought (Wilson & Thomson, 2006).

These include: Henry Fayol (1916); Mary Parker Follett (1920); and Lyndal Urwick (Urwick & Brech, 1946). Perhaps the best summary of the contributions of these and other authors appears in *Writers on Organisations*, now in its sixth edition (Pugh & Hickson, 2007). The book is a good example of how knowledge generated from several original sources can be packaged for educational purposes. In relation to the first edition in 1964 Pugh recounts how he was approached by Morris Brodie of the Administrative Staff College at Henley to produce a booklet to hand out to students introducing them to some of the key management writings (Pugh, 1996). The result was the co-authored book which summarized the leading writers in the field, and enabled students to better understand organizations and their management. Pugh is convinced that *Writers on Organisations* has made a real contribution to management education in the United Kingdom, having sold over a third of a million copies before the sixth edition in 2007.

From the historical perspective it is worth making two observations in relation to the similarities and differences in the section headings used in the first and sixth editions of this publication. First, 'The structure of organisations', 'The management of organisations', and 'People in organisations' appear in both. 'The organization in its environment', 'Decision-making in organizations' and 'Organisational change and learning' are headings not found in the first edition. While too much should not be made of these observations, they do indicate where significant changes have been made in the knowledge base on which management education thrives; namely, the growing importance over a period of 45 years of competition, innovation, environmental change and strategic management.

Secondly, the preponderance of American authors stands out. Of the 22 named authors in the first edition, 11 were American; 18 out of 51 were American in the sixth edition. This American influence in relation to the theory and practice of management is a fair reflection of their impact. But since this publication is intended to be UK oriented, it is appropriate to focus more on British authors as a way of acknowledging their important contributions.

3.2. The Rise of Empirical Management Research

Many of those involved in shaping the body of knowledge disseminated in management education are dependent upon the research and thoughtful leadership of others. Practitioners and consultants modify these 'borrowed findings' in the light of their personal experiences and the information exchanges they share in their professional and work-related networks.

Stalwarts of the classical model of scientific management, such as Lyndal Urwick and Edward Brech, are exemplars of this type of contribution. Based on his army experience as an officer in the First World War, and subsequently as a manager and a consultant (he founded Urwick Orr and Partners in the 1930s, now part of Price Waterhouse and Coopers), Urwick published various papers in the 1920s and 1930s, and collaborated with a fellow consultant Edward Brech in producing influential books on the principles of scientific management (Urwick & Brech, 1946). These activities were in addition to those already mentioned in Chapter 1, relating to his leadership before and immediately after the Second World War, in persuading governments and other key bodies on the need for formal qualifications in management education.

One of the benefits of academic research is that the beliefs held by practitioners and consultants can be challenged/supported on empirical grounds. Two historically important studies will illustrate this. One of the acknowledged weaknesses of 'scientific management' is the tendency for its promulgators to assume that its principles apply to most organizations. From 1953 to 1957 Joan Woodward carried out a pioneering study of manufacturing firms in South East Essex, consisting of a survey of 100 firms followed by an in-depth study of selected firms (Woodward, 1958). The findings showed that there was no one best form of organization. Factors determining the best form included: the objectives of a firm (as reflected in its choice of products and markets) determine what kind of technology (e.g. mass, batch or process techniques of production) it uses; technology in turn determines the best organizational forms (e.g. levels of authority in management, degree of flexibility in the definitions of duties and responsibilities). These 'contingency' findings were also found in a more qualitative study carried out by Burns and Stalker in Scotland (1961). They were able to show that successful organizations matched their organizational forms according to the dynamic nature of the environment in which they operated. Companies operating in an environment characterized by technical innovation appear to require an organizational form which was 'organic' in nature, i.e. more flexible so that they are better able to adapt to unstable conditions. In contrast, companies operating in fairly stable environments adapted by developing a more 'mechanistic' organizational form (e.g. clear hierarchy of control, each manager having clearly defined tasks etc.).

The finance for these and other pioneering studies was provided by the Department of Science and Industrial Research (DSIR), and the findings disseminated by a series of pamphlets designed to be easily read by practitioners. These studies, together with those of the Industrial Administration Research Unit at Aston, made an impact in the United States as well as the United Kingdom. Other research carried out without government funding proved no less influential. Most prominent in this category was the work of the Tavistock Institute of Human Relations, founded in 1946. For example, in using an action research approach (i.e. generating knowledge by combining research and consultancy) Fred Emery and his colleagues were able to show that in the process of designing work systems managers have the opportunity of meeting social as well as technical needs — hence their socio-technical systems model (Emery & Trist, 1960; Trist, Higgin, Murray, & Pollock, 1963). The outstanding early success of the Tavistock Institute in making theoretical contributions based on consultancy work has not been repeated in recent years. One of its recent strategies for survival has been to introduce a degree qualification for one of its more prestigious courses — an MA in Advanced Organisational Consultation. Since 2000 this MA degree, which is based mainly on project work, has been validated by City University London.

Somewhat earlier another institution has contributed significantly to the relevant knowledge base; this was the NIIP founded in 1921. The NIIP initiative was the brainchild of Charles Myers (Director of the Psychological Laboratory at Cambridge). In 1919 he gave a lecture entitled 'Psychology and Industry' in which he identified four areas in which psychology could be profitably applied to industry and commerce: fatigue, movement study, vocational guidance and management (Myers, 1920). Under 'management' Myers included psychological issues of industrial discontent and restricted output, the psychological advantages of different methods of payment and supervision and other conditions which affect the efficiency and the happiness of the workers. Myers and one of his staff at Cambridge, Bernard Muscio (university demonstrator in experimental psychology), were both committed to showing how the scientific discipline of psychology could benefit industry. In one of his published lectures Muscio refers to the First World War:

> The War, among its many unexpected effects, seems to have brought about a popular realization of the material advantages to be derived from the systematic application of science. It taught us many economic facts of which we were ignorant before; and seemed to show that the systematic application of science to industry was chiefly responsible for Germany's considerable industrial development. The war situation forced people to ask what exactly was meant by and what was possible by means of applied science. Even the conservative mind began to consider whether it would not be advisable, in view of the probable immense consequent advantages, to apply science systematically and persistently (1920).

In the 1920s and 1930s research/consultancy activities at the NIIP soon broadened out beyond fatigue and working conditions, and encompassed consumer psychology, job satisfaction, attitude surveys, selection, vocational guidance and training methods (Blain, 1971). In 1932 *Ten Years of Industrial Psychology* was published. The following extract demonstrates two things: there was a need for the application of this knowledge base; the model of a hospital medical school for the advancement and application of this applied discipline was appropriate.

> In 1920 the staff consisted of the present Principal and Director — Dr Myers and Dr Miles. By 1930 it numbered about fifty persons, including some thirty-five investigators, research workers, departmental heads and their assistants — practically all of them university graduates. The general scope of the Institute's work was planned on lines similar to those of a hospital medical school; the Institute would engage in practical work, research, and teaching, none of which could be effectively carried out singly by an organised body, apart from the two others. The practical work was to consist in undertaking investigations into the improvement of the human factor in factories, etc., in introducing better methods of selecting the workers best fitted for vacant positions, and in advising young people as to the careers for which they were most suited. The research work was to include the study of the human conditions necessary to give optimal output, the conditions of mental and muscular fatigue and boredom, and the devising of tests and other methods for the better vocational selection and guidance. The teaching was to include the establishment of a library, propaganda work among employers and employed, training courses, and university and other lectures (Welch & Myers, 1932).

NIIP's output in terms of research and consultancy has been well documented in the *'Occupational Psychology' Journal: Jubilee Volume* (Blain, 1971). The impact of the Institute on Industry, Government and the Universities is considerable when one takes into account not only their 'consultancy' influence on organizations, but also the subsequent activities of their trained staff in other employment situations. Examples of the latter abound as former staff played a key role in selection, training and the assessment of morale within the armed forces, the civil services and business, and in the their contributions to university courses in LSE, Birkbeck, Birmingham, Liverpool, Glasgow etc. (Raphael, 1971). The extensive publications of the NIIP are a reliable record of this accumulated knowledge (Frisby, 1971).

In the mid-1960s the NIIP expanded rapidly following support from the Ministry of Technology. The subsequent withdrawal of this funding, the rising competition from young consultancy firms, the rising influence of industrial sociology, and the growth of business and management education in colleges and universities, all combined to contribute to a financial crisis at NIIP. It suspended activity in 1973; tried to survive on a smaller scale with the help of North East London Polytechnic; but finally closed in 1976. As Derek Pugh points out (personal communication) one of the important additional factors explaining the folding of the NIIP is that members where not prepared to encompass the development of the field from 'industrial psychology' to 'organizational behaviour'. The slow breakdown of traditional mental sets is touched upon below.

3.3. Challenges to Traditional Management Attitudes

Historical examinations reveal the slow changes that take place in management attitudes as new knowledge is disseminated. Beliefs that are no longer reinforced by accepted knowledge weaken over time (Skinner, 1976). Similarly, beliefs incompatible with new knowledge will weaken over time (Festinger, 1957). For example, an assumption underlying Taylor's concept of 'scientific management', and shared by the majority of practitioners over many years, is the belief that the average worker is motivated by 'a fair day's work for a fair day's wage' and little else. Drawing on available knowledge in 1960 the American psychologist and Professor of Management at MIT, Douglas McGregor, argued in a very readable and practitioner-oriented book that the treatment of employees were likely to be influenced by whether management shared a set of beliefs he labelled 'Theory X' or one he labelled 'Theory Y' (McGregor, 1960). Beliefs associated with the former included: the average individual inherently dislikes work and avoids it when possible, and therefore management needs to stress productivity, introduce incentive schemes, and denounce restriction of output; this dislike of work means that individuals need to be coerced, controlled and directed to achieve organizational objectives; the average individual prefers to be directed, wishes to avoid responsibility and seeks security above all. The motivational assumptions under 'Theory Y' include: the expenditure of physical and mental effort in work is as natural as play or rest; individuals will exercise self-direction and self-control in the service to which they are committed; the most significant reward that can be offered in order to gain commitment is the satisfaction of the individual's self-actualizing needs; the average individual learns to accept and to seek responsibility under the proper conditions; more people can contribute to the solution of organizational problems than do so; the potential of the average person is not being fully used. Staff–line relationships under these two philosophies will be quite different: under the former staff departments will be perceived as serving top management to control the line; under the latter they will be perceived as providing professional help to all levels of management.

A second example, while related to the empirical studies influencing McGregor, emerged more forcefully from the research of the Tavistock Institute in London (Trist et al., 1963) and the Work Research Institute in Oslo. Essentially these applied research programmes were generating new concepts about the nature of work (e.g. 'autonomous work groups', 'industrial democracy'). Although their findings were compatible with the findings of other research centres in the United States, the conversion of this knowledge into practice was a slow process because of the conflict they generated among different stakeholder groups (e.g. workers, managers, trade unions, shareholders). But the guidelines emerging from this knowledge, and the underlying values they represented, were sufficiently attractive to motivate individuals, groups and public bodies to build networks and structures to promote their messages. Thus, behavioural and social scientists wrote readable books showing the relevance of this body of knowledge for managers and organizations; e.g.: *Management and the Social Sciences* (Lupton, 1966); *The Manager's Guide to the Behavioural Sciences* (Brown, 1969). Albert Cherns, the Secretary to the Heyworth Committee that recommended the setting up of the Social Science Research Council (Heyworth, 1965), obtained a grant from the newly formed Council to establish the 'Centre for Utilisation of Social Science Research' at Loughborough University. The Centre's four objectives were to research the utilization of social sciences, promote the use of existing social science knowledge, describe the relationships involved in the utilization of social science and work towards a theoretically relevant description of the utilization process (Appleby, 1972) (Cherns, 1979). Cherns held the first Scientific Secretaryship of the SSRC before he was appointed to the first Chair in the Social Sciences in the United Kingdom at Loughborough.

A further vehicle for transforming 'work' to become better aligned to current knowledge in the social sciences was the Department of Employment's 'Work Research Unit'. This unit facilitated dissemination and application of relevant knowledge through researching best practice, consultancy, leaflets, talks and conferences. The activities mentioned so far, together with a host of others, became associated with the quality of working life (QWL) movement. The QWL movement became self-perpetuating as applications, e.g. the replacement of assembly lines by work groups at the Volvo plant in Sweden, were visited by groups of British managers. QWL change programmes were seen by some (particularly in the

United States) in the 1970s and 1980s as a solution to declining productivity and Japanese challenges (Skrovan, 1983).

The third example relates to the attitudes of senior managers towards effective managerial behaviour (particularly 'leadership') and the extent to which it can be changed through formal learning experiences. The phrase 'leaders are born and not made' represents a belief widely held in the nineteenth and the first half of the twentieth centuries (Brech, 2002). The gradual accumulation of knowledge resulting from research on individual differences and managerial competences, and on the selection of managers and leaders, enables one to better understand the relationship between inherited abilities (e.g. 'intelligence') and abilities gained through learning and experience (e.g. interpersonal skills). We now accept that most individuals with an appropriate level of intelligence can learn to become effective managers and leaders, although some will always be 'better' than others. This belief lies at the heart of business and management education, and is the raison d'etre of business schools.

3.4. Forces Leading to Attitude Change

Attitude change can also be thought of as a cultural process that takes place overtime as the build-up of forces for change gradually overcome the forces against change. This model of countervailing forces was initially put forward by Kurt Lewin (1951) to account for attitude changes as revealed in his social psychological studies. Since the turning point of management education via universities was in the early 1960s in the United Kingdom, it is worth illustrating the use of the force-field model in this context by identifying some of the positive forces for change that influenced the thinking of individuals in positions of power (these are listed in Box 3.1).

3.5. Formal Learning Methods Used to Facilitate the Transfer of Knowledge to Management Practitioners

The last item in Box 3.1 brings one back to the core mission of management education. Those individuals involved in the early days of management departments and business schools were very much at the beginning of a learning curve in the United Kingdom. Some were able to visit business schools in the United States to learn from their experiences (Williams, 1974), others had to rely on the shared experiences of their peers at home. A facilitating agent in this context was undoubtedly the *Association of Teachers of Management* (ATM and later AMED — Association for

---

Box 3.1.   Examples of driving forces that changed the context of management education in the early 1960s.

- The efforts of pioneers and leaders such as Lyndall Urwick and John Bolton.
- Colleges and polytechnics successfully engaging in business studies degrees, and in diplomas in management.
- The awareness of UK governments that action was needed to improve the productivity of the United Kingdom for competitive reasons.
- The success of the 'business school' model from the United States, and related models of independent institutions in the United Kingdom (e.g. Henley).
- The Robbins Report (1963) and the Franks Report (1963) reinforcing the need for management education and the role of business schools.
- The success of the Foundation for Management Education in generating money from industry and government (Nind, 1985).
- The existence of relevant institutions or structures able to co-ordinate and represent the interests of their stakeholders (e.g. British Institute of Management, Federation of British Industry).
- The accumulation and dissemination of a body of knowledge relevant to the role of individuals in general management and/or in a special branch of management (e.g. finance and accounts, personnel, marketing, production).

Management Education and Development), founded in 1960 by a group of interested specialists in universities, technical colleges and industry. One of its early publications was *The Academic Teaching of Management* (Pugh, 1966). In the Foreword to the book Pugh states:

> The purpose of the association is the study and appraisal of management education with a view to raising the professional standards of its members. In particular the Association has the aim of providing means for the communication of developments in teaching, relevant research findings and the exchange of experience.

In the Introduction he places the responsibility for developing the profession of management squarely on the shoulders of the teachers of management. Part of the process of improving the academic content and standard of management education is the sharing of information, and hence the organization of the symposium from which the publication was the result. Leading experts were asked to describe how they introduced their subject to

---

Box 3.2.   Subjects covered in management degrees in the 1960s.

- Accounting and Financial Management (Harold Edey, LSE)
- Economics and Econometrics (Maurice McManus, Birmingham University)
- Applied economics (J. R. Parkinson, Belfast University)
- Marketing (Grigor McClelland, MBS)
- Organisation and Methods (John O'Shaughnessy, Cranfield)
- Law (W. F. Frank, Lanchester College of Technology)
- Government (William Mackenzie, Manchester University)
- Industrial Relations (George Thomason, University College Cardiff)
- Communication (Michael Hall, Aston University)
- Behavioural Analysis of Organisations (Peter B. Smith, Leeds University)
- Industrial Sociology (Williams H. Scott, Royal College of Advanced Technology, Salford)
- Personnel Management (Enid Mumford, Liverpool University)
- Operations Research (Edward D. van Rest, Cambridge University)
- Industrial Engineering (Samuel Eilon, Imperial College)
- Management Theory (Derek Pugh, Aston University)
- Business Policy (Raymond Thomas, Bristol College of Science and Technology)

---

students of management (assuming graduates but in disciplines other than the one they represented), and to provide a detailed syllabus, a reading list and specimen examination questions. The subjects covered are listed, together with their authors (and institution in 1966), in Box 3.2. It must be remembered that most lecturers teaching management at that time found themselves in an unfamiliar situation; they were used to lecturing to students coming to learn about the discipline in which they were experts. Lecturing to students, from a variety of disciplines, wanting to learn about the multidisciplinary area called business or management was a new challenge. Any opportunity to gain confidence by sharing ideas with fellow academics struggling with similar challenges was welcomed!

In 1971 Thomas Kempner edited a *Handbook of Management* (1971). He saw the various categories of knowledge likely to be included in a degree aimed at business and management (both undergraduate and postgraduate) as: relevant parts of the social sciences applicable to management — economics, psychology and sociology; quantitative aspects of management (including statistics, operations research and computer applications); functional areas such as marketing, production/operations, personnel/ human resource management, accounting and finance; and the integrating and future-oriented areas of business policy and strategy. Those academics lecturing on management courses in the 1960s and later will acknowledge that these categories have been fairly consistent over time, although some of their labels may have changed. Kempner was the founding director of the Management Centre at Bradford University in 1963; he subsequently became Principal of the Administrative Staff College at Henley and Director of Business Studies at Brunel University.

Maximizing the benefits of management education is dependent upon the validity of what is taught, and the effectiveness of the learning processes employed. Both content and process will be affected by available knowledge, the characteristics and expectations of students, the needs and expectations of employers, and market conditions. All these factors may change over time and from one culture to another. Thus, in terms of content there is less on Industrial Relations today than in the 1960s and 1970s, while international and cross-cultural issues have grown. Similarly, how things are taught has changed over time, as our knowledge relating to adult learning has deepened.

As we have seen there were several factors that held back management education in the United Kingdom relative to some of our competitors. One was the widely held belief that management education attached to universities would be too theory driven and insufficiently practice driven. This may have been partly a carry over from the highly successful 'apprenticeship' method of training that had dominated the British scene for several centuries, but it also reflected the fact that very few British managers in the first half of the past century had had experience of higher education. One of the results of the growth of the business school industry (i.e. the schools and their associated regulators and representatives) is that this anti-academic attitude is now less visible in relation to content than process. In other words, business schools have been criticized by employers and students for some of the learning methods employed. There are two sets of historical observations to be made in relation to this issue: First, a whole range of learning methods have been created to replace the heavily criticized traditional lecture; secondly, difficulties of transferring learning from the 'classroom' to the job have resulted in exploring the benefits of extending the 'individual' learning unit to that of the 'group' and even the 'organization'.

A whole range of learning methods are now in use in business schools. The traditional 'lecture' is no longer the dominant method for transferring knowledge to students. The assumption being made by the lecture is that students are highly motivated to listen to 'experts' in order to share their knowledge and understanding, and thereby to become more effective managers. Under rare circumstances this is undoubtedly true, but dissatisfaction with lecture 'overload' has led to the development of a variety of more active learning methods. The *case study technique* is most closely associated with Harvard Business School (HBS) which introduced it in the early 1920s. The technique required students to study a case written up to illustrate problems that may arise in an actual business setting; in class the expert/facilitator would pose certain questions to generate a discussion. A variation was to form groups of students to generate their solutions to the problems posed, and then nominate a spokesperson from each group to report their findings to a plenary session. The following extract is taken from Christensen of HBS who has extolled the virtues of the case method more than any other person:

> We believe that when educational objectives focus on qualities of mind (curiosity, judgment, wisdom), qualities of person (character, sensitivity, integrity, responsibility), and the ability to apply general concepts and knowledge to specific situations, discussion pedagogy may well be the most effective approach. Lectures about judgment typically have limited impact. Reading about problems or memorizing principles does little to prepare the practitioner-architect, doctor or manager-to apply concept and knowledge to the complexity of real life problems. Discussion teaching achieves these objectives better than alternative pedagogies. It puts the student in an active learning mode, challenges them to accept substantial responsibility for their own education, and gives them first hand appreciation of, and experience with, the application of knowledge to practice (1987, p. 3).

The development of *business games* was an attempt to replicate in the classroom elements of the work situation; these simulations have become more popular with the ready access to computer technology.

Sensitivity training or Training-groups (T-groups) was another import from the United States, although their development in the United Kingdom was also influenced by the experiences of the Tavistock Institute in rehabilitating soldiers from the Second World War (Whitaker, 1965). T-groups grew out of research into group dynamics, and relate to methods of sensitizing individuals to interpersonal relationships in small groups (Bradford, Gibb, et al., 1964). The approach aims to get people to feel and behave differently, and accordingly focuses on the 'here and now' in an interactive group learning situation.

More and more educators realized that effective learning came about when active learning methods were combined with the rich learning resources present in group settings, particularly when participants came from different organizations and cultures. Thus, Henley, for instance, became known for the use of the *syndicate method* of learning, where individuals with experience of management in different settings form small groups to discuss a given issue (often introduced by a distinguished guest). Individuals in the groups take turn to play the roles of 'chair/spokesperson' and 'secretary', thus practicing additional elements of a manager's role. It is not easy to trace the origins of this method of learning but there is evidence that something very similar was used at the military Staff College at Camberley in the 1920s (Rundle, 2006). A similar approach was also used in the United States where it was referred to as the 'Conference method'.

Another example of a group approach stems from the enthusiastic innovative mind of Reg Revans. From being a physicist at Cambridge in 1935 he held various managerial posts before becoming an academic at UMIST, where he was made professor of industrial administration from 1955 to 1965. His research and teaching experiences in management led him to promoting *Action learning* for experienced managers (Revans, 1978). The approach encouraged managers to learn by using their own collective expertise to identify and solve real business problems they were facing. An important feature of the technique was the group setting in which the learning occurred. Revans was so convinced that this approach was right, rather than the traditional one in which the professorial expert played a key role, that he resigned from his Manchester post and operated as an independent consultant. His low opinion of the way in which business schools were developing in the United Kingdom is reflected in the alternative meaning he attached to the MBA concept — Moral Bankruptcy Assured! Nevertheless, his influence on management education in the United Kingdom and the United States has been substantial, he has even had an American university named after him (Teare & Prestoungrange, 2004).

John Morris acknowledges his debt to Revans' ideas in describing The *Joint Development Activity (JDA)* he introduced at MBS. He adopted a version of action learning by using live projects as a major element on their programmes (Morris, 1977). He became the first Professor of Management Development in the United Kingdom; Manchester University thus recognizing his pioneering work on JDA as an effective method on management programmes. Morris describes the basic concept of a joint development activity as: 'the activity is a project-based form of management development work within a single enterprise, using real management issues within the enterprise as the focus for development in project team working. The members of the team are drawn from different functions and locations, and seldom from a natural work group' (Morris, 1977, p. 22).

Care must be taken not to assume that any particular business school was the original 'inventor' of a particular learning method. Some may have become closely associated with a school as a result of the consistent promotion of a particular method and/or because a prominent academic actively marketed the approach. While certain learning methods have become associated with given institutions, it is fair to say that other business schools in the United Kingdom were using similar methods 1960s onwards. This was partly brought about by the exchanges taking place between academics at meetings of the Association of Teachers of Management, at national and international conferences relating to management education and development, and of course by the dissemination of 'good practice' by publication. Also it is worth remembering that in the 1960s (and probably before) the feature that often differentiated a postgraduate diploma from an MSc was a project, and this meant that most MScs/MBAs in the early business schools would have included an assessed project of some kind.

It was not only in management education that learning methods were under scrutiny. As early as 1961 widespread concern over University teaching methods (particularly at undergraduate level) led the UGC to appoint a committee under Sir Edward Hale to review the situation. The following extract is from the foreword written by Chairman of the UGC, Sir John Wolfenden in 1964:

> The report starts from the standpoint that the main object of an undergraduate course should be the development of a student's capacity to think for himself and to work on his own. From this point of view it examines the effect on undergraduate education not only of the various teaching methods in use (such as lectures, discussion periods, laboratory work, field classes) but also of the setting in which this teaching is given and of the examinations to which it leads (Hale, 1964).

The observation is made in the report that the actual content of what is taught at the undergraduate level is less important than at the postgraduate level, where the applicability of the content is more likely to be important. The traditional lecture followed by discussion was still viewed as the dominant method to use. This review came too early for attention to be drawn to the rich and diverse learning methods emerging from management education at both the undergraduate and postgraduate levels.

The conclusion to draw from this brief overview of methods used in management education in the United Kingdom include: there has been a decrease in the use of the lecture as a method in the transfer of knowledge, and an increase in the use of more active methods of learning such as simulations, learning in groups and carrying out live projects. This shift from the passive to the active in the management context is now supported by most authorities and research findings (Kolb, 1984).

The evaluation of education and training is a problematic area. While it is possible to assess learning taking place during a programme in terms of specific knowledge and skills, it is very difficult to evaluate a programme once the participants have returned to their normal jobs. Studies attempting to do this have met with disappointing results. Transfer of learning failure has usually been explained by the discrepancy between the 'new' learning and the 'culture' of the organization in which a person's job is embedded. This knowledge encouraged some organizations to favour developing whole teams rather than individuals, and some to go even further and extend the learning unit to multiple teams or to whole organizations. The label 'organization development' or OD is often used to categorize this approach to learning and change. The substantial knowledge that has accumulated in the development of OD programmes has been applied through management consultancies rather than business schools (Blake & Mouton, 1964). But the learning model such programmes generate has influenced executive development pro-grammes delivered by business schools, particularly the tailor-made ones (e.g. Williams, 1980). Corporate-based management education has already been briefly touched upon in an earlier section (i.e. Section 1.6). It is inappropriate to go any further into the extensive literature on OD, organizational learning and change. This knowledge is relevant where the primary purpose of a management development programme is to bring about change within an organization, rather than to educate managers more generally so as to enhance the economic activity and productivity of a nation.

3.6. Structures for Encouraging and Improving the Quality of Research

Research that has implications for management education has been financed from a variety of sources. Foremost have been the government research councils, e.g. DSIR and its successors the SSRC and the ESRC. Foundations and grant-awarding bodies have made significant resources available, including: Ford Foundation, FME, Leverhulme, Nuffield and the King's Fund. Government agencies such as the UGC and the Higher Education Funding Council have enabled universities to carry out relevant research. The 'users' and 'disseminators' of management research, such as corporations, professional bodies and management consultancies, have also made significant contributions by commissioning or sponsoring research.

The growth of management as a credible academic discipline initially came about as a result of the relevant inputs made by several longer established disciplines, such as economics, psychology, sociology, political science, mathematics etc. Only some of these were sufficiently recognized in the early part of the twentieth century to have been given departmental status within universities, to have named degrees, and to have associated learned societies and professional bodies. These developments within a discipline have rested on their success in advancing a given area of knowledge, and this in turn has rested heavily on the quality of their research. In the early days of the 'management movement' it was the engineers, psychologists and others, trained in the scientific method, who appreciated the practical importance of quality research. Those academics and industrialists responsible for ensuring that the development of management education in the United Kingdom should be part of the university system, also appreciated the value of the 'critical academic mind-set'.

Management as a discipline and a profession is still at its formative stage. As we have seen various factors came together after the Second World War to favour the emergence of management education within the higher and further education systems. The establishment of LBS and MBS was intended (among other things) to advance the development of quality research relevant to management. This was a key criterion in the appointment of professors. At the same time FME and DSIR were also supporting research initiatives at other business schools. Additional early forces driving quality research were generated by CUMS and ATM. When the latter became less concerned with research and more with teaching, training and consultancy, there developed a need for a body which would ensure that business schools in the United Kingdom had the necessary support for developing and maintaining quality research in management. The leadership of a group of individual scholars initiated moves for such a body to emerge when it was most needed.

3.6.1. British Academy of Management (BAM)

We have already referred to AMED, CUMS, AMBA and ABS as significant non-governmental institutions in the development of business and management education in the United Kingdom. BAM is another institution to be added to this category. Its 20-year history has been written by Peter McKiernan. The idea for the institution grew out of an informal gathering of UK scholars attending the American Academy of Management (AoM) in San Diego in 1985. They 'lamented the lack of a multidisciplinary association in the UK, where folks could share ideas from their respective disciplines' (McKiernan, 2008, p. 2). The group challenged Cary Cooper to do something about it (at that time he was based at UMIST), and BAM was duly formed in 1986. This was exactly 50 years after the foundation of AoM; an institution that provided yet another model for the United Kingdom, albeit after a long time lag.

As McKiernan points out there were several forces at work to encourage the formation of BAM. They included: the rapid growth of business and management courses in the universities and polytechnics since the 1960s were not matched by the supply of research-oriented teachers; the growing gap between the number of academics in business and management education and the amount of ESRC research money going to them as opposed to other categories in the social sciences; the threat/opportunity of the redirection of research money as a result of the first RAE in 1987; the evolution of the ATM from an institution primarily representing academics to one increasingly representing consultants and trainers; by the mid-1980s the UK-based *Journal of Management Studies* (founded by Grigor McClelland at Oxford in 1963) had acquired an international reputation but there were few other outlets for quality papers in the United Kingdom.

The impetus for the formation of BAM was provided by senior professors of management (e.g. Cary Cooper, Andrew Pettigrew, Roger Mansfield, Andrew Thomson, David Otley, Enid Mumford, David Weir), who drew up an outline for the new academy and persuaded their respective business schools to financially support the first conference to be held at the University of Warwick in 1987. The original aims of BAM as listed in McKiernan were as follows:

- To encourage the sharing and development of a research knowledge base for all management disciplines.
- To act as a forum for the various disciplines in management and to encourage the development of an integrated body of knowledge commensurate with management as a profession.
- To encourage and promote disciplinary research and collaboration among the various management disciplines.
- To further the development of management education in the United Kingdom.

The founding principle was to focus on management research and not teaching or consultancy. Subsequent activities have emphasized BAM's role in the training and development of research students and faculty, and in generally uplifting the quality of management research.

Even while its membership was relatively small, and its office facilities minimal, BAM began to influence events. In 1991 it criticized MCI's attempt to restructure management education in the United Kingdom, following on from the Handy Report and Constable/McCormick Report and the creation of the NCVQs. In particular, it criticized the low benchmarks for the standards, and the inadequate recognition of the role of knowledge and understanding. Underlying these criticisms was the inherent conflict between the perspectives of academics and professional management about 'research relevance'. This conflict was further debated in BAM's dealings with ESRC. One of the startling findings in an analysis of the distribution of ESRC research grants was the serious underfunding of management research. 'In 1988/89, seventy-six proposals were submitted to the ESRC by researchers in business and management studies. This was the largest from any discipline. But only nine grants were awarded — a success rate of only 12%. This compared with those in economics, politics and sociology of 48%, 40% and 36% respectively' (McKiernan, 2008, p. 4). Subsequent discussions within BAM (recognizing weaknesses in the quality of some submissions) and ESRC (recognizing the biases that may have been operating against management research) led to the setting up of the Commission on Management Research by the ESRC, chaired by George Bain (Bain, 1993). While most of the recommendations in the report were accepted by BAM and ESRC, a number of issues remained unresolved, including the criteria for 'relevance'. The diversity of opinion within BAM (exacerbated by different research orientations of the old and newly created universities in 1993) led to a re-examination of its mission and strategy. What emerged was heavily influenced by the thinking of Ken Starkey and David Tranfield: 'to position management research within the social sciences in a way equivalent to the position of engineering in the physical sciences or medicine in the biological sciences i.e., that management research was transdisciplinary and has to be informed by practice as well as concepts and theories' (Starkey & Tranfield, 1998).

Gradually during the 1990s a pattern of activities developed and this was accompanied by a steady growth in BAM membership and a strengthening of the secretariat. Developments included annual conferences, doctoral workshops, the launch of *The British Journal of Management* in 1990, the introduction of the fellowship grade in 1993, an expansion of its role into teaching (since research informed teaching and vice versa) and the formation of special interest groups (SIGs) in 1999. Links with ABS grew, and new links were formed with various international bodies to the mutual benefit of members; e.g. the AoM, the European Academies of Management (EURAM), the Australian and New Zealand Academy of Management (ANZAM). For various reasons progress was temporarily halted at the turn of the century, but BAM restructured itself and appointed a permanent administrator (Clare Saunders) located in offices shared with ABS. Since 2002 BAM has been in a better position to offer an improved service to its members, and to exert greater influence in national affairs. In recent years BAM has joined other learned bodies to form the Academy of Social Sciences. Academicians are distinguished scholars and practitioners from academia and the public and private sectors. It responds to Government and other consultations on behalf of the social science community, as well as facilitating interactions that promote social science and enhance its value to society.

3.6.2. Public Funding Body for Management Research: SSRC/ESRC

These bodies have already been mentioned above but their influence on the development of knowledge relevant to management education needs further clarification. The *SSRC/ESRC* had considerable influence on research conducted by business schools and the social sciences generally. Perhaps its main contribution has been through its attempts to facilitate the generation and application of research findings through research structures and processes. This aim is understandable given that it is a public body and therefore aware of its need to defend the funding it receives from the government. A second main contribution stems from its 'research council' function — it has a duty to promote and maintain 'excellent standards' in research. As Caswill and Wensley have shown these dual goals are not always compatible (2007). Their brief history of the Council covers the period when it was formed (1965 as SSRC, from 1982 as ESRC) to the present time. They identify four key episodes to illustrate the underlying conflict between rigour (displaying appropriate scientific norms in generating knowledge as judged by academic peers) and relevance (displaying practical relevance as judged by managers likely to be making use of this knowledge):

(1) The action research model of the Tavistock Institute (founded in 1947 mainly from a long-term grant from the Rockfeller Foundation). The model typifies close interactions between researchers and users during the research project. Theoretical guidelines were originally provided by the work of Kurt Lewin (1951).

(2) The establishment of an Industrial Relations Research Unit at Warwick University in 1968. This represented the SSRC early attempt to set up directly employed units, and it had a distinctive 'pluralistic' governance. 'IR research succeeded in institutionalizing itself and its core practices. Senior IR practitioners sat on the relevant subject committee and also on the SSRC Council. The Council continued to fund a IR unit (later a 'centre') at Warwick and sustained it until the end of the century. IR journals were established and continue today' (Caswill & Wensley, 2007, p. 298).

(3) The business school phenomenon is one of the major ways in which academics and users engage with each other. As pointed out earlier, NEDO saw management education as a key in achieving higher economic performance. It pushed this perspective in various reports, e.g. (Rose, 1970).

(4) In the 1970s the Council adopted a more 'initiative-based' approach, as exemplified by its 'Open Door Scheme' of 1977. The idea here was to involve non-academic institutions and potential users at the formulation

stage of a research project, so that they would be more interested is using the findings. 'But the Open Door Scheme experience illustrated that a clear focus on a rather different and diverse group of users raises issues of quality and criteria, and suggests that there can be no dominant criterion of disciplinary rigour. User engagement seems to create particular problems of evaluation' (Caswill & Wensley, 2007, p. 305).

In the 1980s it was clear that management research was not receiving its fair share of funding from the social sciences pot, and this led to the suggestion among BAM members for a separate Council for management. The chances of this coming about were remote; but the continued pressure from BAM and ABS led to the setting up of the 'Commission on Management Research' in 1993 to consider the funding and impact of social science research in business and management. The Commission was chaired by George Bain, who was at this time Principal of LBS (and for a number of years earlier was Director of the IR Research Unit at Warwick). 'The Commission's report focused on two central issues: the need to recognize that research in the management field faced the so-called twin hurdles of relevance and rigour; and the need for a more defined and strategic forum, tentatively labeled a Management Research Forum, in which the priorities for management research could be discussed and resolved' (Caswill & Wensley, 2007, p. 305). The Forum failed to develop into anything useful, not surprising given some earlier attempts at similar moves.

An ongoing event described in the Caswill and Wensley paper concerns the interactions between management research and its utilization. This began in 2001 when the Council approved a management research initiative (AIM) 'to develop the UK's management research to a world class level, relevant to business in the UK and European Union'. This reflected the continuing concern that management research was not contributing enough to United Kingdom's economic performance.

Caswill and Wensley conclude in their paper that in spite of the relative success of the Tavistock and IR communities in embedding the processes of knowledge transfer and exchange in their everyday work, the 'rigour supporters' remain unconvinced. The rigour/relevance argument may have moved forward (Starkey & Madan, 2001), but the inherent tension involved continues into the future.

3.6.3. *Council for Excellence in Management and Leadership*

ABS (and BAM) played an important part in influencing a key body in effectively achieving its mission. In April 2000 the CEML was appointed by the Secretaries of State for Education and Employment and for Trade and Industry to develop a strategy to ensure that the United Kingdom has the managers and leaders of the future to match the best in the world. The Council was chaired by Sir Anthony Cleaver, but the initial membership did not have an individual with direct experience of a UK business school (Sir Martin Sorrell had been through Harvard). Only after representations from ABS was Professor Stephen Watson (then Principal of Henley) made a member of the Council. The work of the Council was carried out by several working groups including those representing: organizations, professions, SMEs, higher education, non-higher education. The extensive consultations and research carried out identified a significant mismatch between the need for management and leadership skills, and their demand and supply. The 30 recommendations made stem from a strategy the Council recommended to Government 'a strategy whose rationale lies in the explicit link which we make between good management and leadership and performance' (CEML, 2002a).

The Council formed, under the chairmanship of Stephen Watson, the Business School Advisory Group in the summer of 2001 to develop proposals relating to management and leadership provision at the higher education level. In their report they list five broad objectives: stimulating the demand for management education and training; strengthening the application of knowledge and the development of leadership skill within management education; improving access to continuous management learning for practicing managers; strengthening the knowledge base and knowledge transfer; resourcing and marketing the business schools (CEML, 2002a). Several recommendations are made under each objective, and it is those under the fourth objective that are most relevant to this section. Here emphasis is given for the need of business schools to provide leading-edge thinking to issues relevant to companies, and knowledge transfer from researchers to practitioners should be given high priority by those commissioning and evaluating research. The key players expected to implement these recommendations are listed as: business schools, ESRC and Management Initiative Research Forum, Engineering and Physical Sciences Research Council (EPSRC), employers, BAM. The following section deals with an initiative stemming from these recommendations.

3.6.4. *Advanced Institute of Management Research*

AIM was established in 2002 in order to increase the contribution of world class UK management research. Financial support is provided by the

ESRC and the EPSRC. Their introductory leaflet includes the following objectives:

'To ensure our projects shape effectively management practice of the future, our four objectives are to:

- Conduct research that will identify actions to enhance the UK's international competitiveness.
- Raise the quality and international standing of UK research on management.
- Expand the size and capacity of the research base for UK research on management.
- Engage with practitioners and other users of research within and beyond the UK as co-producers of knowledge about management'.

In pursuit of these objectives they have identified three broad research themes: UK productivity and performance for the twenty-first century; sustaining innovation to achieve competitive advantage and high-quality services; adapting promising practices to enhance performance across varied organizational contexts. The main structure created to fulfil these objectives is an AIM research community of fellows and scholars that ensure that a wide variety of approaches are covered and findings are disseminated through AIM-initiated workshops, publications and events. AIM Executive Committee was initially Chaired by Sir George Bain and directed by Professor Ann Huff for the first year; currently it is Chaired by Professor Dame Sandra Dawson (Judge Business School and now Deputy Vice-Chancellor, University of Cambridge) and directed by Professor Robin Wensley (Warwick Business School), with Professor Andy Neely as Deputy Director. The main stakeholders are represented in the executive committee which is the governing body. Over the past seven years AIM has developed a high profile with its well-publicized events and publications. The latter include executive briefing brochures such as: *The Future of Business Schools in the UK* (Ivory, Miskell, et al., 2006), and *Leadership of Business Schools: Perceptions, Priorities and Predicaments* (Ivory, Miskell, et al., 2008); also academic publications such as *The Challenge of Business-University Collaboration: Context, Content and Process* (Bradley, Gregson, et al., 2004) and *The Search for Talent and Technology* (Bruneel, D'Este, et al., 2009).

In the 1980s it was shown that research activities could account for the greater expenses involved in educating undergraduates at universities than in polytechnics and colleges of higher education. This led to the idea of introducing the RSE in 1986, so that larger research grants went to those institutions assessed to produce more high-quality research. As Morris points out 'The start of the RSE in 1986 did much to legitimize business and management research in the eyes of university vice-chancellors, courts and senates. The designation of this subject area as a unit of assessment meant that it was recognized as a respectable area of academic enquiry which could attract research funding which in turn could be spent within the institution at the discretion of its senior managers'. (2010). The research quality ratings of some institutions were better than expected (e.g. UMIST) and others worse (e.g. MBS). Leaders of business schools decided to play the system when it came to the 1989 RSE, by emulating the practices of the highest scoring departments at UMIST and Warwick. The expansion of the higher education sector in 1992, with the polytechnics becoming universities, meant that a change was necessary in the main criterion of assessment (from the best of five publications by all academic staff in the unit of assessment in the past three years, to the best two to three produced by each member of research active staff in the past three years). The 1992 exercise was named RAE. Changes were introduced in successive RAEs to make the process more manageable and acceptable (e.g. more weight being attached to refereed journals of high standing). RAEs were carried out every few years, in 1996, 2001 and 2008, and determined the amount of research funding going to universities (and by implication to business schools). The financial incentive no doubt had an effect in improving the quality of research within schools as measured by the criteria being applied. It also had unexpected consequences such as high salaries being offered to entice research 'stars' to new employers, and the significant effect RAEs have on the reputation of business schools because of their incorporation into the criteria the media (e.g. *Financial Times*) use for ranking schools nationally and internationally.

3.7. Knowledge Growth and Consolidation through Academic Journals Based in the United Kingdom

One way of tracing the development of knowledge relevant to management education is to identify the foundation of those academic journals that represent the disciplines and content of courses run by business schools, particularly multidisciplinary programmes such as the MBA. Again the focus will be on quality UK-based journals with a national and international readership. Corresponding journals are published in several other countries, particularly in the United States which has dominated this pool of knowledge for many years. Besides 'quality' and UK-based, the other factors determining the selection of the sample discussed below include: historical importance; prestigious organ of a learned society; representative of a subject area central to management education.

The *Journal of Occupational and Organisational Psychology* (*JOOP*) is now in its 83rd year of publication. Originally entitled *Journal of the NIIP*

(1922/1923–1930), followed by a succession of changed titles: *The Human Factor* (1932–1937), *Occupational Psychology* (1938–1974), *Journal of Occupational Psychology*, to its current title in 1992. Each of these titles reflects changes in the development of knowledge, the dominant contributors, the readership and the owners. The insertion of 'Journal' in the title in 1975 was to emphasize its standing as an academic journal of a learned society (the British Psychological Society took over the journal in 1975); the inclusion of 'organisational' in the title in 1992 was to reflect the representation of the subject in business schools and university management departments rather than in departments of psychology. In an analysis of papers the journal published in the five-year period 1989–1994 it was shown that: 34% came from overseas 'management' departments, 23% from overseas psychology departments, 25% from UK business schools or management departments, 7% from joint authors in departments of management and psychology, and only 11% from authors in UK psychology departments (more than half of these authors came from the ESRC-supported 'Social and Applied Psychology Unit' at Sheffield) (Shimmin & Wallis, 1994).

The *Journal of Management Studies* (*JMS*) was the first academic journal in the United Kingdom to cater specifically for those researching and teaching within the field of management. Prior to its publication corresponding journals were almost exclusively American. The first volume appeared in 1964. The Society of Management Studies (now the Society for the Advancement of Management Studies) was established as a charity the previous year. The opening paragraph in its original Memorandum of Association states: 'The object for which the Society is established is the advancement of education in the field of management studies'; it goes on to specify its powers to edit, publish, pay authors, to hold lectures etc., pay for research, and to award prizes. A prime mover in the establishment of JMS in 1963 was Grigor McClelland, while he was Management Fellow at Balliol College, Oxford, and before he became Director of MBS. In the areas of organization theory, strategic management and human resource management JMS has become one of the most influential management journals in the world.

Human Relations was founded in 1947 by the Tavistock Institute of Human Relations in London and the Research Centre for Group Dynamics at MIT in Boston. Its objective was to encourage theoretical and methodological contributions to the social sciences and through their integration to promote their practical application in solving society's problems. The history of the journal and the changes in its fortune over time are the basis of an interesting paper by three former editors (Loveridge, Willman, et al., 2007). The founding and evolution of the journal was built around three interconnected strands: the creation of the Tavistock Institute and its inter-organizational alliances in the United States, facilitated by a long-term grant from the Rockefeller Foundation (reflecting the outstanding reputation of the founders to take 'action research' to help in the reconstruction of British industry); the creation of Tavistock Publications in London as a means of communicating to scholars and practitioners; the foundation of the journal to be published by Tavistock Publications with joint British and American editorship. In the earlier volumes papers were published by scholars that have made an impact on management thinking and organizational researchers, including Eric Miller, Eric Trist, Fred Emery, Chris Argyris and Douglas McGregor. Papers that have become classics in the organizational behaviour literature include: 'The representation of labour turnover as a social process: studies in the social development of an industrial community (the Glacier Project)' (Rice, Hill, et al., 1950); 'Some social and psychological consequences of the Longwall Method of Coal-getting: an examination of the psychological situation and defences of a work group in relation to the social structure and technological content of the work system' (Trist & Bamforth, 1951); 'The causal texture of organizational environments' (Emery & Trist, 1965).

The authors point out that the 1970s governments in the West were becoming anxious about failing productivity and poor labour–management relations in manufacturing industries. Applications of the Tavistock's innovative concepts were reflected in government-sponsored 'QWL' and 'industrial democracy' programmes in various countries. While the early momentum ensured that the number of manuscripts submitted to the journal increased, the impact of the work Institute changed as several of the original pioneers moved abroad or into consultancy. The 1970s onwards have proved to be a difficult financial and organizational period for the Institute, although the journal has successfully survived. Since 2000 noticeable changes have occurred in the editorial team, e.g. the 'Tavistock Institute membership of the team ended, indicating the intellectual parting of the ways that had been underway for some time' (Loveridge, Willman, et al., 2007, p. 1884). A consequence has been a reduction in the number of papers associated with one of the roots of the Tavistock, i.e. psychodynamics. But 'It has retained distinctiveness in a number of ways. ... Not tied to any academic society or academy, it can sustain a Catholicism of approach to the innovative, creative or unusual contribution to academic debate' (p. 1886).

Long Range Planning (*LRP*) was first published 40 years ago. Not only is it the longest running journal devoted to strategic management, but its editorial policy is to span both academic research and practical concerns. A recently published paper on the history of LRP conveys the story of the development and changes associated with the relatively new management discipline of business strategy (Cummings & Daellenbach, 2009). The authors analysed the themes, topics and issues covered in the 2366 articles published in LRP from 1968 to the end of 2006. Six key words were present in the titles in significant numbers across the 40 years: corporate; organization; merger, acquisition, joint venture and divestment; creativity and innovation; technology; change. The authors state:

> Combining our key word data from LRP titles and abstracts enables us to interpret strategic management's most constant (and so perhaps its fundamental) themes, as process and practices relating to the corporate whole, the organizing of resources and how the corporation responds to or manages change. Thinking more broadly, one could add to this set responses to or decisions about technology and other related environmental issues, and the recognition of the importance of creative or innovative developments. Over 40 years, these appear to be strategic management's essential elements, and so actions, thinking or decisions related to one or some combination of these issues may be confidently defined as 'strategic' (Cummings & Daellenbach, 2009, p. 239).

In contrast to these key words/themes the authors list the many 'fads' that have come and gone, or failed to reach their threshold of constancy, such as: Delphi; portfolio analysis/planning; vision/mission; best practice; scenario planning; TQM/quality circles; business process reengineering; the value chain; balanced scorecards; cognitive mapping; management by objectives. In addition, the authors identify some themes that appear to be on the rise, e.g.: knowledge and learning; networks and relationships; culture; corporate social responsibility and business ethics. They link the first three to the resource-based view of the firm (searching for sources of competitive advantage that cannot be readily replicated by others), and the last to the greater awareness of the influence of organizations on the wider social and ecological environments. One of the apparent discrepancies in the papers they explore is the domination of the use of 'strategy' over the use of 'planning'. This change from planning to strategy is seen as the 'strategic manager's distinctive contribution to business thinking and practice'. Planning is seen as part of strategy, the latter straddling the ground between the firm and the wider economy and society. Another trend identified is the decline in the promotion of 'prescriptive tools, models and theories' in favour of cultures, processes and practices, thereby recognizing the uniqueness of an organization and the value of frameworks and cases.

The *Journal of the Operational Research Society* replaced the title *Operational Research Quarterly* in 1978. It was first published in 1950 as the disseminating arm of the scientific meetings of the Operational Research Club which was founded in 1948. In 1954 'club' became 'society'. The origins of this learned society, and indeed of the discipline of operations research or management science, grew out of the Second World War when teams of British scientists (e.g. physicists) were able to demonstrate the value of applying scientific methods to arriving at optimal solutions to operational problems in the military setting (Gaither, 1986). Their success influenced the development of the discipline in the United States when that country entered the War. The expertise developed was transferred to non-military applications after the War, and as illustrated in an earlier section the discipline became part of management education.

The *British Journal of Management* (*BJM*) is one of the youngest UK scientific journals devoted to management. It was launched in 1990 as the journal of the BAM, and reflected the dissatisfaction of many British academics at the apparent 'bias' of many American or American-influenced journals. It met a need for the growing number of academics in business schools and management departments in the United Kingdom and abroad. It publishes papers across the full range of business and management disciplines, and has become a highly ranked journal.

In order to promote the advancement of education and research in the areas of accounting and finance, the British Accounting Association (BAA) publishes the refereed academic journal *British Accounting Review*. The BAA was established in 1947, and has about 780 members. There are of course many other learned bodies with academic journals but some of these publications are too specialized to become involved in management education. For example *The Economic Journal* which is the prestigious journal of The Royal Economic Society, a body founded well over 100 years ago and currently claiming a membership of some 3000 members.

With the growth in management education and related research the market for several of the above journals has expanded significantly. As Huw Morris points out 'the money-generating potential of these new business and management journals was increasingly evident from the late 1960s onwards. Indeed, in 1970 a group of academics from the Management Centre at Bradford University established their own journal publishing company named MCB (now Emerald Press) after their department. With an initial stake of £500 of share capital each, they launched a string of what would become highly profitable journals' (2010, p. 11). Barrie Pettman, part of the first cohort of MSc students in 1966 at the Graduate Business Centre (now Cass), was one of those who made his first million through MCB. He shares some of the reasons for his success in the book entitled *What Self-Made Millionaires Really Think, Know and Do* (Dobbins & Pettman, 2002).

3.8.   Observations on the Growth of Knowledge-Based Management Education

This topic has been tackled from several different perspectives in the course of answering the three questions: What does this body of knowledge consist of? How was the quality of this body of knowledge monitored and improved? What learning processes facilitate the acquisition of this knowledge? In the context of this book it is only possible to touch on these issues. They are nevertheless important since at the end of the day the reputation and effectiveness of management education, and therefore business schools, rests on this body of knowledge. Illustrations of topics discussed have intentionally a UK flavour, otherwise the rich American sources would have swamped the content.

The paucity of relevant knowledge in the eighteenth and nineteenth centuries is at first sight surprising, until the scenario is viewed in the context of the time. As the scientific mind-set gradually replaced philosophical armchair thinking, a new world opened up which was to prove valuable to 'managers' operating in an increasingly competitive and changing world. Historically, the American example of Frederick Taylor and scientific management proved pivotal but others in Europe were also influenced by the same factors as Taylor. In the United Kingdom the two World Wars provided a step change in the application of empirically based knowledge to the solution of managerial problems. The thrust or 'leadership' provided by such individuals as Charles Myers, Lyndall Urwick, Fred Emery, Joan Woodward, Tom Burns and George Stalker, Derek Pugh and colleagues proved influential. But this influence would have much weakened without government and institutional support, hence the mention of such bodies as various government departments, the NIIP, Tavistock Institute, DSIR, Aston University, SSRC/ESRC etc.

A phenomenon that is well known, and has been the subject of research, is the slow process in which the utilization of findings occur (Cherns, 1979; Caswill & Wensley, 2007). Some examples have been included above. Historically the most obvious is the traditional belief held by many top managers in British industry in the nineteenth and early part of the twentieth centuries that leaders are 'born and not made'. Forming and changing managerial attitudes or mind-sets of this nature are a slow and complex process. Since this is the business that management education is in, it was relevant to explore some of the historical events such as the formation of the Association of Teachers of Management and the various learning methods used on courses.

Finally, this chapter has explored the structures for encouraging and improving the quality of research influencing thinking in management education. Here the public funding bodies have played a key role; e.g. DSIR, SSRC, ESRC, Higher Education Funding Council for England (HEFCE). Academia has also been a major player through the formation of learned bodies (e.g. BAM), and the creation of peer-reviewed journals (e.g. BJM). It now remains to explore the success of the above historical developments in terms of the national and international standing of UK business schools.

Chapter 4

The Standing of UK Business Schools

The major providers of business and management education in the United Kingdom today consist of business schools, professional associations and management consultancies. Of these, the business schools have dominated the scene since the 1960s. The penultimate part of this history will therefore focus from this period to the present day.

As was mentioned in earlier sections academic interventions in management education occurred at the end of the nineteenth and beginning of the twentieth centuries. But these were relatively minor activities of some universities. It was only in the 1960s that several universities founded 'business schools' as we know them today. Box 3.1 listed key driving forces that helped to bring this about. How a selection of schools developed is briefly outlined in the case studies below. A ready criterion for recognition as a business school is membership of ABS. The membership criteria, as agreed at the 2008 AGM, are applied by the Executive Committee when considering an application; these are reproduced in Box 4.1. At the moment over one hundred institutions fall within this category (see Appendix 2 for an up-to-date alphabetical list). Institutions given 'associate status' are done so at the discretion of the Executive Committee; they do not have voting rights. Examples of institutions in this category are those interested in business and management education but may not meet all the necessary criteria, accrediting organizations or overseas institutions.

One of the outstanding developments in the United Kingdom since the 1960s has been the growth of the 'business school industry'. With the help of HESA statistics, ABS was able to include in the 2008/2009 annual report the following figures relating to business and management education for the past 13 years (this is the period for which comparative data were available):

- The number of undergraduate students studying for a degree in the United Kingdom has increased by 29% while those studying business and management have grown by 66%.

Box 4.1.   ABS membership criteria.

Membership is available to institutions which are universities, colleges, schools or any other bodies which satisfy all of the following criteria:

- Delivery in the United Kingdom of higher education level qualifications in the business and administrative studies area as defined by HESA;
- Have gained formal approval from the Privy Council and either approval by the QAA or QCA/SQA for their qualifications;
- Demonstrable commitment to research or scholarship in relation to their qualifications.

In considering the third criteria and whether an institution can demonstrate a commitment to research or scholarship, the following will be taken into account: the institutional strategy and policies, the quality and quantity of published outputs, and the existence of and support for the 'community of scholars' associated with the qualifications.

- The growth in postgraduate taught degrees (e.g. MBAs and specialist masters in finance, marketing and HRM) has been 80% over the same period. More than 53,000 full-time equivalent students were registered in 2007/2008.
- The growth in postgraduate research degrees has been almost as impressive, even though smaller numbers are traditionally involved. The 83,000 full-time equivalent research students attending UK universities in 2007/2008 represent 41% increase over the past 12 years. During the same period, business and management has grown twice as fast, with 4300 full-time equivalent registered in 2007/2008.
- In the year 2007/2008, almost one in seven of all students were studying business and management in the United Kingdom.
- The international nature of management education in the United Kingdom is revealed when analyses show that 30% of business and management students come from outside the United Kingdom, and 25% from outside the European Union.

Another way of studying the remarkable rise in the 'business school industry' is to examine the relative standing of the schools with the help of media rankings.

4.1. The Relative Standing of UK Business Schools

In the early 1960s the variation between business schools was considerable. This was probably most marked with respect to research performance, but they also differed as to whether they catered for postgraduates, postgraduates and undergraduates, or just undergraduates. As this sector of higher education became more mature, institutional influences started to operate (e.g. AMBA, ABS, AACSB and EFMD), and new market forces emerged (e.g. MBAs were in demand, as were bachelors in business studies, and masters in specialist aspects of business). With the growth of the service industries and decline of manufacturing industries, more school leavers and graduates were attracted to aspects of business and management as demonstrated above.

To compare the standing of business schools nationally and internationally, a credible yardstick is required. Since the most prestigious international ranking exercises are those produced by the *Financial Times*, these have been selected as the main framework to explore this area. The *FT* rankings and listings do not extend to undergraduate programmes, but some useful information on these programmes is provided by the Guardian.

The order of institutions in Table 4.1 needs to be clarified at the outset (the *FT* full-time MBA global appeared in 25 January 2010; the others appeared in relevant *FT* issues during 2009). The ordering of the first group of 13 schools was determined by their average ranking over the past three years (i.e. 2008/2009/2010). The next group of three were not ranked in the top 100 in all three years in question, but their rank for 2010 has been placed in brackets. The next group of three schools have not as yet appeared in the top 100 on account of their full-time MBA degree, but they have been ranked in the top 95 on the basis of their part-time Executive MBA degree for 2009. The next group of eight have been ranked according to the listing of their Online MBA degree (i.e. the larger the numbers graduating the higher the rank received). The final group consists of a single institution since so far it only appears in the MSc rankings.

Rankings can be controversial for very good reasons — they are based on criteria reflecting the choice of a group of experts. It is therefore important to understand the criteria behind rankings. Details of the methodology used can be found on the *FT*'s website. The essentials are: to be considered for inclusion a school must be accredited by one of the accepted bodies (e.g. EQUIS), have had a full-time MBA degree for at least 4 years, cohorts of at least 30, and first graduated class at least 3 years ago; information collected from alumni via a questionnaire (e.g. weighted salary, placement success rank, recommended rank, international mobility rank); and from schools via a questionnaire (e.g. per cent employed at 3 months, per cent of women faculty, per cent on international board, international experience rank, *FT*

Table 4.1: *FT* rankings.

Business schools in UK	MBA global	MBA executive	MBA online listing	MSc management
London Business School	1	8		
Judge Business School, University of Cambridge	16			
Saïd Business School, University of Oxford	18			
Lancaster University Management School	24			
Manchester Business School, University of Manchester	31		3230	[44]
Cranfield School of Management	30	33		
Warwick Business School, University of Warwick	36	35	1718	
Imperial College Business School	35	31	360	[33]
Cass Business School, City University	41	21		16
Strathclyde Business School, University of Strathclyde	41	78	250	[27]
School of Management, University of Bath	80			35
Bradford School of Management (TiasNimbas Business School)	76	79	633	44
University of Edinburgh Business School	75			
Aston Business School, Aston University	[73]		80	20
Durham Business School, Durham University	[74]	88	523	33
Birmingham Business School, University of Birmingham	[75]			
ESCP Europe		25		3
Henley Business School		44	4093	36
Ashridge Business School		52		42
Edinburgh Business School — Heriot-Watt University			8503	
Open University Business School			6150	
University of Liverpool Management School			2162	
School of Management, Royal Holloway, University of London			609	
Resource Development International — University of Wales			481	
Oxford Brookes University Business School			318	
Aberdeen Business School			193	
University of Surrey — School of Management			88	
London School of Economics and Political Science				3

doctoral rank); the research rank is developed by counting the number of papers published in 40 specific academic and practitioner journals in the past 3 years. The weightings given to various elements, and adjustments made for school size, are defined. The rationale behind the *FT* business school rankings and some of the problems encountered in their preparation, has been written up in a publication (Bradshaw, 2007).

Further rankings produced by the *FT* include executive education programmes in the context of 'open' and 'customized' courses. The rankings presented in Table 4.2 are again for the past three years (the latest years at time of writing are 2007/2008/2009). Schools included must have achieved a minimum of annual income as determined by the *FT* (this accounts for the few business schools included).

Two further tables need mentioning to adequately cover the nature and standing of UK schools. Table 4.3 covers the MSc degrees within the broad area of finance; these and other specialist masters have grown significantly over the past 20 years. The order of schools in the *FT* tables has been kept for convenience and no ranking is implied. It is worth pointing out that most schools have an MSc in finance; the number of such programmes in any school varies from 1 (e.g. LBS, Said, Cranfield) to 6 (e.g. MBS, Cass, Durham), and the number of full-time students from any single school ranges from 53 (Judge and Cranfield) to 439 (Cass).

Table 4.4 shows the *FT* European business school rankings for UK schools. Again it is the three-year average rank that is shown. Where this is not available for a school then their 2009 ranking is in brackets. The detailed methodology for the ranking process is more involved because of the necessity of combining the rankings from different exercises (see www.ft.com/businesseducation). This 'ranking of rankings' takes into account the full-time MBA (January 2009); the open enrolment and customized non-degree executive education programmes (May 2009); masters in management degrees (September 2009) and executive MBA (October 2009). Schools must appear in at least two of the four ranking exercises to be considered for inclusion in the *FT* European rankings. Only one UK school (two if ESCP Europe is included) appears in the top 11 positions; France and Spain are both well represented. In the next 30 the United Kingdom performs well — 15 appear. In the next 29, 3 appear. This means that 19 (20 if ESCP Europe is included) UK business schools have made the top 70 in the *FT* European ranking exercise. Only those that have three-year averages have been included in these figures. Two interesting findings from the full table as published is the consistency of the ratings for each school from one year to the next, and the fact that UK and French schools make up for more than half the top 70 (the number ranked by the *FT* in this exercise).

Table 4.2: *FT* rankings of non-degree programmes.

Business schools in UK	Executive education 2007/ 2008/2009	
	Open	Customized
London Business School	13	25
Judge Business School, University of Cambridge		
Saïd Business School, University of Oxford	[28]	35
Lancaster University Management School		44
Manchester Business School, University of Manchester		
Cranfield School of Management	28	20
Warwick Business School, University of Warwick		59
Imperial College Business School		
Cass Business School, City University		
Strathclyde Business School, University of Strathclyde		
School of Management, University of Bath		
Bradford School of Management (TiasNimbas Business School)		
University of Edinburgh Business School		
Aston Business School, Aston University		
Durham Business School, Durham University		
Birmingham Business School, University of Birmingham		
Leeds University Business School — Nottingham Business School		
ESCP Europe	32	
Henley Business School		
Ashridge Business School	11	
Edinburgh Business School — Heriot-Watt University		
Open University Business School		
University of Liverpool Management School		
School of Management, Royal Holloway, University of London		
Resource Development International — University of Wales		
Oxford Brookes University Business School		
Aberdeen Business School		
University of Surrey — School of Management		
University of Exeter BS		
University of Southampton School of Management		
London School of Economics and Political Science		
School of Management, University of St Andrews		

Table 4.3: Number of finance-related MScs in 2009, and student totals.

Business schools in UK	No. of finance-related MScs	Full-time	Part-time
London Business School	1	146	68
Judge Business School, University of Cambridge	2	53	
Saïd Business School, University of Oxford	1	61	
Lancaster University Management School	3	138	
Manchester Business School, University of Manchester	6	217	
Cranfield School of Management	1	53	
Warwick Business School, University of Warwick	3	217	
Imperial College Business School	3	245	25
Cass Business School, City University	6	439	79
Strathclyde Business School, University of Strathclyde	4	135	70
School of Management, University of Bath	1	84	
Bradford School of Management (TiasNimbas Business School)	2	99	
University of Edinburgh Business School	2	71	
Aston Business School, Aston University			
Durham Business School, Durham University	6	286	
Birmingham Business School, University of Birmingham			
ESCP Europe	1	64	
Henley Business School			
Ashridge Business School			
Nottingham Business School	1	158	
Edinburgh Business School — Heriot-Watt University			
Open University Business School			
University of Liverpool Management School			
School of Management, Royal Holloway, University of London			
Resource Development International — University of Wales			
Oxford Brookes University Business School			
Aberdeen Business School			
University of Surrey — School of Management			
University of Exeter Business School	6	377	
University of Southampton School of Management	5	247	1
London School of Economics and Political Science	4	170	46
Leeds University Business School	5	165	
School of Management, University of St Andrews	4	97	

Table 4.4: The *FT* European business school rankings for UK schools (3-year average ranking).

Business schools in UK	Top 70 European business schools
London Business School	2
Judge Business School, University of Cambridge	35
Saïd Business School, University of Oxford	20
Lancaster University Management School	26
Manchester Business School, University of Manchester	37
Cranfield School of Management	12
Warwick Business School, University of Warwick	19
Imperial College Business School	23
Cass Business School, City University	14
Leeds University Business School	54
School of Management, University of Bath	38
Bradford School of Management (TiasNimbas Business School)	34
University of Edinburgh Business School	43
Nottingham Business School	50
Strathclyde Business School, University of Strathclyde	[17]
Aston Business School, Aston University	35
Durham Business School, Durham University	25
Birmingham Business School, University of Birmingham	[61]
ESCP Europe	8
Henley Business School	28
Ashridge Business School	27
Edinburgh Business School — Heriot-Watt University	
Open University Business School	
University of Liverpool Management School	
School of Management, Royal Holloway, University of London	
Resource Development International — University of Wales	
Oxford Brookes University Business School	
Aberdeen Business School	
University of Surrey — School of Management	
University of Exeter BS	
University of Southampton School of Management	
London School of Economics and Political Science	19
School of Management, University of St Andrews	
Sheffield Business School, Sheffield Hallam University	[69]

4.1.1. Undergraduate Business Studies Degrees

It has already been pointed out that undergraduate degrees in commerce appeared in a few universities in the first half of the past century. A noticeable expansion came in the 1960s/1970s when institutions in the Higher Education sector introduced Bachelor degrees in Business Studies under the aegis of the newly formed CNAA. Now 113 academic institutions run such degrees. The *Guardian* newspaper has taken up the lead ranking Bachelor degrees that fall broadly within the business and management studies area. One of the major differences between the criteria used by the *FT* and the *Guardian* is that the latter does not take research performance into account; the argument being that their guide is primarily for first-time students, and therefore it is more important to focus on teaching than research. However, of the 18 UK business schools included in the *FT*'s Top 100 Global MBA rankings for 2010, 11 are placed in the top 22 of the Guardian's list of 113 institutions. Only Aberdeen and Oxford Brookes in the *FT*'s classification do not make the top 22; while Leicester, St Andrews, Exeter, Glasgow, LSE, Reading, Loughborough, Nottingham, Heriot-Watt, Buckingham and Leeds are all included (see www.guardian.co.uk/education/table/2010). The rankings are based on official information published on higher education institutions, collected by the HESA and the National Student Satisfaction Survey.

4.1.2. Some Observations

In studying these tables certain observations come to mind:

- In terms of their international standing, UK business schools are well represented. In terms of the full-time MBA, 10 schools are in the top 50, 13 in the top 100 (16 out of 100 if one considers the 2010 year on its own).
- Schools that were active in the management field in the 1960s have continued to maintain their high standing.
- The performance of LBS has been particularly consistent and impressive.
- The more recently formed Judge and Said Business Schools at Cambridge and Oxford universities, respectively, have moved rapidly up the rankings.
- The UK business schools that appeared in the top 50 MScs in management (a European business school product) also appeared in the top 100 *FT* rankings.
- Specialist MScs in the finance area are not ranked but the number of their degrees under this category is listed, as are their numbers of full-time and

part-time students. A few schools that did not appear in the earlier
ranking tables make an appearance, owing no doubt to their emergence
from departments of economics.

- Some schools shine in both the full-time and executive MBAs as judged by
  the *FT* rankings (e.g. LBS, Cranfield, Warwick, Imperial, Cass, Strathclyde,
  Bradford, Durham), others may be outstanding in one of these categories
  (e.g. Judge, Said, Lancaster, MBS, Bath, Durham, Henley, Ashridge).
  Reasons for this pattern are best understood by exploring a number of case
  studies that have been published on UK business schools.
- UK schools perform well in the *FT* European top 70 rankings, but only
  LBS enters the top 11.

4.2.   Case Studies

Comparative tables of business schools tell us little as to why some
have developed differently from others. To gain insights into the 'why', one
needs to explore their case histories. Unfortunately only a few have
researched and published in-depth histories. Information from these,
together with the skeleton outlines available on others from multiple
sources, has formed the basis of the discussion below. The aim is to focus on
their early beginning so as to better understand the dynamics of business
school start-ups, and the factors contributing to their growth and
reputation. The case studies have been grouped in order to draw out
similarities and differences in the histories. Thus, Henley and Ashridge
illustrate two pioneering and independent 'business schools', initially
reflecting the beliefs of industrialists, but gradually driven to adopting a
more academic orientation in order to survive market changes and
fierce competition. London Business School and Manchester Business
School were created with money from the State and Industry so that two
British 'model' business schools would exist to compete alongside the likes
of Harvard and Wharton. Aston, Cass and Aberdeen are examples of
business schools that have emerged from faculties of engineering. Warwick
is an example of a business school where management education grew out of
industrial relations research and teaching alongside other academic
disciplines when Warwick University was created in a manufacturing
heartland. Judge and Said are two business schools that had to overcome the
resistance to change of two of the world's most ancient and prestigious
universities; their late arrival on the business school scene has not dampened
their success. The Open Business School is unique in the United Kingdom
in adopting the distance learning technology of its parent university for all
its degrees.

4.3. Early Independent Institutions

Henley was the first independent institution in the United Kingdom to be running courses for administrators and managers. The most recent publication relating to its history is that of David Rundle (2006); an earlier history had been written by Harry Slater (1989). A distinctive feature of Henley was that it emerged as the result of a group of senior businessmen coming together at the Reform Club in 1943 to explore the idea of a National Staff College. It was incorporated in 1945 as the Administration Staff College; the first Principal was appointed in 1946 (Noel Hall), and its first courses launched in 1948. Noel Hall and Geoffrey Hepworth (the then Chairman of Unilever) had a major influence on the early development which was geared to short courses with the maximum length of 12 weeks. The philosophy behind their approach was to provide a learning environment which would prepare executives for more responsibility by reflecting on their experiences, and opening up these experiences for comment by co-learners.

An individual who had an important role to play in the initial move that led to Henley was Lyndall Urwick. There is no doubt that in the inter-war years Urwick was the most prominent individual promoting management education in the United Kingdom. One of his early appointments was working with Seebohm Rowntree, head of the York chocolate company and a progressive philanthropist, helping to assist with the modernization of the company. His growing reputation resulted in him being appointed Director of the International Management Institute in Geneva in 1928. In the early 1930s he formed his successful consultancy firm Urwick Orr and Partners. Unfortunately for him, his vision for management education required longer courses than those favoured by fellow founders of Henley; this was probably influenced by his acquaintance with the American business schools. Urwick's interest in being actively involved in the formation of Henley diminished after 1943 when it became clear that he was unlikely to be the first Principal. His continued involvement in management education found an outlet in the committee he was asked to chair by the government in 1945. This committee reported in 1947 and led to the introduction of more recognizable qualifications in management, a development that had been taking root in technical colleges but without a standardized syllabus (Urwick, 1947). By the end of the 1950s, over 60 colleges were offering the newly introduced certificate and diploma in management studies. While this national qualification attracted student numbers it failed to enthuse industrial leaders, and criticisms were levelled at the quality standards achieved.

Returning to Henley. The idea of a staff college had its origins in the Army's Staff College at Camberley which had been established in the nineteenth century. Henley's pioneering efforts in management education extended beyond the United Kingdom by providing a model for others to emulate and by being prepared to offer advice to their founders. The concept of an administrative staff college was readily understood by Commonwealth countries such as Australia and New Zealand. From the early 1950s Henley played a leading part in the development of management education in the United Kingdom (and to some extent the Commonwealth) by hosting meetings, reviewing developments and fostering dialogues among academics. In the early 1960s it sponsored a number of books published by Hutchinson. These were intended to make life somewhat easier for those managers attending the Henley courses by bringing together in a convenient and readable form some of the knowledge that form the basis of good management. Thus, the publication 'On Thinking Statistically' by M. B. Brodie was aimed at making managers more aware of the need to think statistically (1963). Reference has already been made to the book by Derek Pugh and his co-authors — 'Writers on Organizations' (Pugh, Hickson, et al., 1964). Tom Lupton's book 'Management and the Social Sciences' highlighted the significance of social science knowledge to the function of management (Lupton, 1966). Of course students on other courses in the country also benefitted from these publications.

In the early days Henley was distinctly different from the business schools emerging in the United Kingdom in the 1960s. Gradually the increased competitiveness in the sector, and the changing market, pulled it in the direction of university-based schools. The entry of university-based business schools in the market from the 1960s onwards created financial problems for Henley which did not receive the State support provided by the UGC. Developing an association with a university was the coping response selected. Discussions with Brunel University started in 1971 and a satisfactory agreement was reached a year later, while enabling Henley to maintain much of its independence. This new association meant that Henley moved closer to being like other business schools, while preserving as many of the essential values of its founding fathers. For example: its first Masters qualification was launched in 1974; a joint BSc programme with Brunel was started in 1978; in 1979 it appointed its own professors; from 1982 it launched its distance learning and tailor-made corporate MBA programmes; in 1991 Henley received its Royal Charter; in 1997 it awarded its own degrees; the accreditation stamps of approval from AMBA, EQUIS and AACSB followed three years later.

These developments were undoubtedly aided by the appointment of its first 'academic' principal in 1972. Tom Kempner was previously the founding director of Bradford Business School, a school that had flourished under his guidance. The move of Henley towards academia was therefore no surprise. Its new status and activities meant that its original name 'Administrative Staff College' was described by Kempner as 'increasingly inappropriate and confusing'. He was unsuccessful in getting the name changed to 'Henley Business School' but allowed to use the name 'Henley — the Management College' in 1981. The Kempner strategy continued from 1990 under the second academic principal — Ray Wild (also from Bradford) — and in 1991 the name 'Henley Management College' was used. The association with Brunel (from 1972 to 1997) had served its purpose even though tensions had developed as a result of the bureaucratic procedures characteristic of the university system.

However, the greater autonomy achieved by Henley was insufficient in the face of continued environmental change. The school had come a long way from its flagship 12-week general management course that had probably been in decline since 1978 (closed in 1991). Apart from its educational value, this course was also the 'laboratory' for its most publicized research programme. This was the research carried out by Meredith Belbin of the Industrial Training Research Unit into the roles undertaken by members of teams competing with each other in a business game. The research was initiated in 1967 and published in book form some years later (Belbin, 1981). Other research projects were undertaken by Henley over the years but as its fifth Principal Stephen Watson (2001–2004) said, 'we are a teaching-led, not a research-based, business school' (Rundle, 2006). The next step change for Henley was to enter into discussions with Reading University with a view to a merger. In many ways the two institutions complemented each other. The merger took place in 2008 under Christopher Bones, the first business leader to hold the post, who had succeeded Watson as Principal in 2005. Bones was appointed to head the merged school and the identity of Henley was preserved as 'Henley Business School'. It remains to be seen what will happen in the future as an integral part of Reading University.

Ashridge's history has much in common with Henley, and has found it as difficult to thrive under the increased competition created by the university-based business schools. The relevant information for this brief account comes from interviews and publications (Coult, 1980; Sanecki, 1996; Thomasen, 2009). As with Henley, the buildings and grounds had an extensive history before they were used as a base for management education. The property was acquired for an educational foundation in 1928 'for the use of the Conservative Party as a college for the study of politics, economics, civics and related subjects. ... The new college, named in memory of Andrew Bonar Law, Prime Minister in 1922–1923, commenced its working life in 1929' (Coult, 1980). A distinguished body of Governors was formed. The intention of the 'College of Citizenship' was to rely on external speakers with a small tutorial staff. The War saw Ashridge being used as a temporary hospital. This arrangement came to an end in 1948, and the Governors sought to free Ashridge from the constraints of its Trust Deeds (particularly its tie to a political party).

The new Trust Deeds received Royal Assent in 1954. However, by 1956 the Governors realized that the College was unlikely to survive on its programme of short courses unless representatives of industry were prepared to take it over as a going concern. Sir Hugh Beaver, of Arthur Guinness, took the lead in gathering such a group. He was concerned about a proper need for management education and training. He and a group of other powerful industrialists agreed that courses of three to four weeks duration were more acceptable to industry than the 12-week general management course being run by the Administrative Staff College at Henley. It was fortuitous for Ashridge that a group of industrialists were seeking an alternative to Henley just when they were becoming disillusioned with Henley's strategy. From April 1959 the College was launched on its new path — renamed 'Ashridge Management College' to reflect its mission of education for management, accommodation on a par with a good hotel, general management courses of four weeks duration with shorter courses in marketing and accounting.

In 1962 Ashridge appointed Dr Christopher Macrae as Principal. His most recent career was in academia (head of Chesters Residential Management Centre and before that a Professor of Industrial Administration at the Royal College of Science in Glasgow). Ashridge's development now followed a similar path to Henley's following the appointment of Tom Kempner as its principal. 'Dr Macrae's work was devoted to expounding the conviction that the purpose of management training in a post-experience college was to help a person, by means of short courses, to build on his or her own experience to date, to compare it with others from often widely-differing organizations, and with the aid of new ideas and new techniques, assist him to become a better manager. The corollary to this reasoning was that a manager, faced with continuously having to adapt to changing factors, needed the stimulus of fresh courses at various stages of his career. Ashridge developed a series of courses graded for all stages from junior management up to the level of director' (Coult, 1980, p. 17). Various new appointments were made. In 1964 Philip Sadler was appointed as Director of Research thus enabling new courses in the behavioural sciences to be introduced. In 1968 he was appointed Principal. During the 1970s Ashridge benefitted from a series of grants from the FME, no doubt helped by the fact that one of the Governors (Sir John Partridge) was Chairman of the Foundation and thus able to share his first-hand knowledge of Ashridge.

Under Sadler (1968–1989) and subsequent principals (Michael Osbaldeston, 1989–1999; Leslie Hannah, 2000–2003; Kai Peters, 2003 to date), Ashridge survived on the basis of modifying its core products in the face of increasing competition. Short courses for executives in a quality learning environment was the basis for its reputation, but on their own they were not sustainable as the university-based business schools geared themselves to meeting a variety of markets. Given its practical orientation that was well received by the corporate market, its long-standing consultancy research base and the growth of the national and international MBA markets, Ashridge's expansion into MBAs and MSc (e.g. management consultancy) was not surprising. Its readiness to submit itself to rigorous accreditation by universities (e.g. the MBA programme was accredited by City University from 1988) enabled it to demonstrate its ability to meet the criteria for awarding its own degrees by 2008. One of the dilemmas with an accreditation agreement is that the time comes when an accredited institution becomes a more serious competitor, and any mutual benefits present at the start of the relationship can quickly diminish. Although the circumstances were different, the deterioration of the mutual benefits relationship between Henley and Brunel led to a similar parting of ways. As Tables 4.1 and 4.2 showed, both Ashridge and Henley are now serious competitors within the business school sector. The potential weaknesses of prestigious but independent colleges surviving in the management education field are still a struggle in tough economic times.

4.4. Great Expectations for Two 'Model' Institutions

LBS is one of the few business schools to have recorded and published its early history, and the information below is mainly based on this publication (Barnes, 1989). As we have seen, the 1940s, 1950s and 1960s saw a serious interest in management education. This interest had been slowly emerging as a result of the superior economic performance of the American economy with its long-established business schools. Evidence of the increased interest was brought about by a number of factors, including: Lyndall Urwick's committee which published its report in 1948; the founding of the Administrative Staff College at Henley in 1946 by a group of senior industrialists; the forward thinking of other industrialists such as John Bolton (a graduate of HBS and chairman of Solartron) and members of Parliament such as Sir Keith Joseph in 1957 (both these individuals were instrumental in the foundation of the FME in 1960); the conversion of Ashridge to management education in 1959 by a group of senior industrialists; the Robbins Committee in 1963 recommending the creation of two major business schools to supplement the additional developments already underway in some universities and other institutions, and the Franks Report recommending the formation of two major schools associated with London and Manchester Universities. These and other milestones have been identified in Box 1.2.

Since the Franks Report led directly to the establishment of LBS and MBS, it is sometimes referred to as marking the start of management education in the United Kingdom. But as we have seen the management education movement was already well under way. Indeed, Morgan Witzel makes a strong case for this, and claims in his recent book on management history that 'The first "business school" in the modern sense was probably the East India Staff College at Hayleybury in Bedfordshire, established in 1805. ... By the end of the eighteenth century, large portions of the Indian sub-continent had come under the East India Company's direct rule, and the company did not have enough trained administrators ... An early attempt at founding a staff college in India failed, but the governors of the company .... Decided that the idea had merit and resolved to put it into practice in Britain and founded Haileybury to train managers and administrators for the company's service.' (Witzel, 2009, p. 10).

However, the Franks Report does mark the arrival in the United Kingdom of the American concept of a business school. Both LBS and MBS designed their masters to be a two-year programme, and at a fairly early stage they used Graduate Management Aptitude Test (GMAT) as an aid to the selection of students. Emphasis was laid on the appointment of staff with reputations for quality research in the relevant areas of management knowledge and quantitative techniques rather than practical managerial experience.

Principles applied by the first LBS Principal, Dr Arthur Earle, a Canadian businessman, included: appointment of academic staff would be for five years rather than tenured; salaries should reflect what the individual could obtain within and outside academia; and that an average working week would expect from staff two days of teaching, one for research and one for consultancy (Barnes, 1989).

Although the first academic planning board included the heads of Imperial College and LSE, the new school enjoyed considerable autonomy from London University as recommended in the Franks Report. But some drawbacks of being part of London University led LBS to seek a Royal Charter in 1982; this was obtained in 1984. The influences of Harvard could be seen in LBS's use of case studies, and those of MIT in the emphasis on mathematics and quantitative methods. In the early mid-1960s, early senior appointments were made in the area of economics (e.g. Ball, Beesley), quantitative methods (Moore) and finance (Rose). The gap in the behavioural sciences was the most difficult to fill and in the end D. G. Marquis and Victor Vroom had to be recruited from the United States for short periods and Dean Berry for a longer one. It was not until 1968 that Derek Pugh and John Child were recruited from Aston.

LBS was fortunate in developing 'on a greenfield site' with a generous budget. But this brought with it some problems such as the use of temporary accommodation before a permanent home was found. Also, when the second appeal was made by FME in 1970, the funding was shared more widely than LBS and MBS. This underlined the need to become more self-sufficient.

Several centres/institutes formed underlined the research strength of LBS. For example: the Economic Forecasting Centre put LBS on the map with a succession of successful directors who subsequently went on to distinguish themselves in other roles in business and government (Ball in 1967, Burns in 1976, Budd in 1980, Currie in 1988); the Institute of Small Business Management was set up in 1976 to promote teaching and research in entrepreneurial management; the Centre for Business Strategy was established in 1982 to study the processes companies follow in making strategic choices (directors included John McGee from 1984, John Kay from 1986).

As the ranking tables in Tables 4.1 and 4.3 indicate, LBS has always been at or near the top in the national and international contexts. It has fulfilled many of the intentions of the Franks Report and remains one of the top business schools in the world on most counts. Also, in a less obvious way (and possibly less intentional way) it has contributed to the development of other business schools in the United Kingdom by the dispersion of its PhD students and experienced staff to the competition.

MBS has also published a scholarly book on its early history (Wilson, 1992). The initiative that brought it about, i.e. the Franks Report, meant that its progress would inevitably be compared to that of LBS. This comparison is all the more interesting because the founding fathers of MBS were less prepared to follow the traditional American model than LBS (except for the two year Masters rather than the one year recommended by Franks).

Why Manchester as the setting for a major business school? Several reasons, including: it had an established name for its contributions to economics as an academic discipline; the development of management had been encouraged by Teddy Chester when he was appointed as Professor of Social Administration in 1953, having previously been involved in the research programme of the Acton Society Trust; the appointment of Douglas Hague to lead the management faculty (he had been running the post-experience courses in management at Sheffield University); established links between key individuals (e.g. Chester and J. W. Platt — the first executive secretary of FME and director in 1964 — were already acquainted; the Vice-Chancellor Mansfield-Cooper ensured that Franks was fully aware of his support); a well thought out set of proposals were prepared by the University. As Wilson writes: 'It was the critical mass of high quality academics assembled within the University which was of central importance in considering why Lord Franks came to his conclusion in 1963. The team had already generated a wide knowledge not only of understanding business problems and their solution, but they had also extensive experience of running courses ...' (Wilson, 1992).

The 'founding fathers' labelled the early development of MBS the 'Manchester Experiment'. 'The Manchester Experiment can be defined as a highly practical, learning-by-doing approach to management education, undertaken in a democratic, non-departmental organization which was only loosely coordinated at the top'. Moreover, applicants sharing a belief in a multidisciplinary approach were favoured in appointments made. This philosophy was intended to produce a continuous stream of innovation. Unfortunately it produced mixed results, and in later years the history of MBS was characterized by efforts to change its culture so that it could compete more effectively alongside national and international business schools.

Unlike LBS, MBS started life more closely linked to its host university. As already mentioned it was part of the Faculty of Economic and Social Studies, and only in 1968 did it become the Faculty of Administration. It had its own Council in 1964 but this was chaired by the university vice-chancellor, and consisted of 18 members half of whom were internal academics. 'Progressively the Council's role was marginalized by the academics, particularly with respect to broad strategy and course design. Indeed, it was the staff who were more influential in creating the philosophy and structure at MBS, and by the early 1970s the Council no longer played much of a role in the areas Franks had intended it to lead' (Wilson, 1992). The Councils of both MBS and LBS were responsible for the appointment of the directors/deans, but it is noteworthy that the former appointed someone who was an academic and a businessman by virtue of his role in his family firm (Professor Grigor McClelland was appointed in 1965), whereas the latter went for a more traditional businessman (Dr. Arthur Earle was appointed in 1965 and came from being CEO of Hoover). A common factor for both schools was that they were initially housed in temporary buildings — MBS until 1971, and LBS until 1970.

By appointing junior staff on short-term research contracts, MBS managed to avoid the rest of the University practice whereby staff were given tenure after serving a period of probation. But the School remained subject to the UGC's constraint whereby only 40% of staff could be above the senior lecturer level. LBS seemed to avoid this problem since they pushed for greater autonomy from London University at the beginning, and were subsequently more successful in creating endowed chairs. The value system fused into the MBS culture by such individuals as Tom Lupton (a sociologist/anthropologist) and John Morris (a social/occupational psychologist) meant that the teaching approaches employed favoured the learning-by-doing and participative methods (e.g. projects and case studies); and the decision-making and organizational structures developed were based on consensus and an informal communication network rather than a traditional system based on a hierarchical structure. Wilson recounts McClelland 'In his own words, he believed he was a "facilitator", arguing that it was the character, rather than the quantum, of his leadership which was more important in developing what was described as "a federation of self-starters". It was an approach which symbolized the informality of the School, and the "founding fathers" regarded this as a major contributing factor in explaining the willingness to innovate at all levels, elaborating a distinctive approach to management education which they claimed was setting MBS apart from competition' (Wilson, 1992).

Certainly one thing that MBS became known for in the early years was the Joint Development Project. This has already been described (see Chapter 3), and owed much to the thinking of Reg Revans of 'action learning' fame. A drawback of the School's success in the learning sphere is that it emphasized its practical image to the disadvantage of its academic research image. Somehow the School failed to develop a balance of the two, with the result that while it was drawing in much needed income from its short courses, recruitment to the MBA programme was falling short. Its failure to reach the target student figures set by Franks drew in criticisms from the UGC and FME for devoting too many funds to organizational experiments and resource intensive teaching methods. Moreover, its fading research image was unhelpful in the recruitment of research stars, and this was reflected in the 1988 average research quality rating (i.e. 3) it received in the first Research Assessment Exercise.

As early as 1970, when the School was expanding, a lack of cohesion developed. Stafford Beer was asked to carry out a review and to make recommendations. His report evoked considerable discussion, but Tom Lupton and most of the staff were against his proposals. The end result was that two school-wide committees were created — an 'operations group' and a 'development group'. In the early 1970s the School went through various financial difficulties, but these improved after 1975 thanks mainly to the post-experience short courses and the company-specific courses. Research grants also picked up in the 1980s. In the 1970s and the early 1980s the divergent research achievements between MBS and LBS were clear, the latter receiving twice as much research grant income than the former as well as having a superior publication record and twice as many researchers. The School became more aware that a culture change was needed; in other words to distance itself more from the strategies of the founding fathers and to move closer to the academic priorities of some of its competitors. Factors enabling this change to occur included: staff committed to the idea of MBS being a top business school in Europe; change of personnel (McClelland left in 1977 and within 4 years Hague left to Chair the ESRC; John Morris left to run his own consultancy firm); in 1983 Business School Council decided not to extend Lupton's contract beyond 66 years of age; staff pressing for change (they were concerned over the growth of company-specific programmes); the new Vice-Chancellor, Sir Mark Richmond, instituted a review to be carried out by a member of the University Council (Sir George

Kenyon); acting director (Professor R. Stapleton) modified the internal structure to strengthen control from the centre; the accounting system was brought more into line with the University system; the School's Policy Group brought out a clear mission statement in 1983, emphasizing the School's desire to locate its image 'towards the academic end of the management education spectrum'.

Tom Cannon was appointed director in 1989. Following the Jarratt Report (Jarratt, 1985) a more professional approach to management was introduced in the School (e.g. refinements to the management structure, planning to include a continuous revision of strategic and operational aims). Each member of the Faculty was allocated to one of five discipline groups: accountancy and finance, business economics, operations and information management, HRM, marketing and strategic management. The intention was to introduce a matrix system of management. One of Tom Cannon's aims was to see MBS becoming a 'research-driven enterprise'; another was to gain greater autonomy for the School from the University (the Kenyon Report recommended a strengthening of the links!). In 1991 MBS Council agreed to a proposal to convert the Faculty of Business Administration into a limited company with charitable status — this was a similar status to that enjoyed by LBS. But Cannon was unable to persuade the staff and the University to support the proposal. On leaving MBS he became CEO of the newly established MCI. One counter proposal at that time was the idea of a federal organization encompassing MBS, the School of Management at UMIST, and the Faculty of Economics and Social Studies at the University. This in effect is what happened when Manchester University and UMIST merged in 2004.

To complete the story of MBS it is therefore relevant to include some details of UMIST and its School of Management. UMIST was originally The Mechanics' Institute (1824–1882), the institute was upgraded through a series of title changes. In 1956, as the Manchester College of Science and Technology it achieved independent university status under its own Royal Charter. In 1966 it changed its name to UMIST and all non-degree courses moved to Manchester Polytechnic (now Manchester Metropolitan University). Since 1905 the institute was part of the Faculty of Technology of the University of Manchester, and as UMIST it was academically part of the university but financially and administratively independent. From 1993 it had full autonomy with power to award its own degrees. When the two universities merged in 2004, UMIST had developed a strong School of Management. This slight diversion from MBS story allows one to observe that in the 1920s the antecedent of UMIST was one of the pioneering academic institutions in management education with the formation of a Department of Industrial Administration, funded by an endowment from asbestos magnate Sir Samuel Turner (Tweedale & Hansen, 2000).

Torrington's history of the School of Management dates the earliest structure of the School as 1918 (Torrington, 2002).

The mergers that took place in 2005 have resulted in the 'new' Manchester Business School (with its teaching staff of more than 200) becoming the largest campus-based business school in the United Kingdom. MBS may yet come close to challenging LBS as the premier business school in the United Kingdom, and meet the expectations originally expressed in the Franks Report.

4.5. Management Education Emerges from an Engineering Context

Both *Aston* and *Cass* business schools were hosted by universities that grew out of institutions with Colleges of Advanced Technology (CATs) status. They received CAT status in 1956/1957, and gained university status when all the CATs were awarded their Royal Charters in 1965/1966. The source for the historical information relating to *Aston* is mainly taken from the School's 60th Anniversary publication (Teeling & Filby, 2008). The birth of Aston Business School was earlier than Cass. Courses in industrial administration had in fact been running since 1928 at the then Birmingham Technical College. In 1947 a separate Department of Industrial Administration was established 'with its aim to extend facilities for study and discussion of current techniques and problems in industrial management to all levels of interest in this field, and thereby to make some contribution to the maintenance of high standards of management practice in the Midlands' (Teeling & Filby, 2008). The inaugural lecture in the department was given by Lyndall Urwick who was regarded as one of the most prominent management consultants in the United Kingdom (Chairman of Urwick Orr and Partners). Urwick made a further contribution in that the findings of the study group of engineers he led, as part of the British-American collaboration to learn about management education, formed the first publication of the department.

The CAT status awarded in 1956 attracted a number of academics who subsequently distinguished themselves. Lupton was awarded a large DSIR grant; he persuaded Derek Pugh to move over from another department in the college, and in 1961 the Industrial Administration Research Unit was borne. The output of the Unit became known as the 'Aston Studies' because of the pioneering approach to the measurement and explanation of organizational structure. The Unit has had an impressive publication record, and most of the researchers involved subsequently achieved professorial status beyond Aston (Pugh, 1996).

In 1972 the Department of Industrial Administration became the Management Centre. By now it was offering a full range of undergraduate, postgraduate, research and post-experience courses. A major difference between Aston and Cass was that the former included undergraduate degrees at a much earlier stage; also the MSc in Industrial Administration replaced the Diploma in the subject at a later stage (i.e. in 1975). The MBA label replaced the MSc from 1978. In the same year the Management Centre occupied a new building; financial constraints meant that it had to be occupied before its completion as planned. Aston had to wait until the deanship of John Saunders (1997–2007) before a £20 million extension to the Nelson Building was complete in 2006.

In the early 1980s all universities suffered from severe financial cutbacks imposed by the Thatcher government. Despite redundancies across the university (academic staff decreased from about 1000 to 500), the Management Centre's research capability was significantly augmented by the import of research active staff under the university's restructuring. The early research culture developed by the Industrial Administration Research Unit continued to benefit the Centre. A Work and Organisation Research Centre was established in 1983 with a 5-year grant from the ESRC and additional centres were created in subsequent years. As with Cass, specialist MSc degrees often grew out of research centres. In 1987 under the deanship of John Child the Management Centre was renamed Aston Business School, and in the same year a distance learning MBA programme was introduced. During the latter half of the 1990s several new MSc courses were launched; a phenomenon that occurred across many business schools as they strove to remain financially competitive. By 2007 Aston was running around 15 specialist Masters. With the wide choice of business schools available in the market in the 1980s and beyond, reputation became a key factor determining student recruitment. Judging reputation is not something that is easily done by potential students, except for the very top business schools (e.g. LBS). To enable the market to make an informed choice several accrediting bodies were established; in the United Kingdom these are AMBA, EQUIS and AACSB. Aston is one of the few business schools to be accredited by all three bodies. As we have seen media rankings also play a powerful role in determining reputation. Assessment criteria taken into account by these bodies and some of the media include results achieved in the QAA visits and in the RAE.

Cass Business School shared similar problems to Aston, but its developmental pathway revealed significant differences. Before the formation of the department that eventually became Cass, management education had a formal presence in the Department of Social and Industrial Studies. This department had been formed on achieving CAT status in 1957 to continue to ensure that all students followed a course in liberal studies and some instruction in the principles of industrial organization. In 1961 Alvin Leyton was appointed the Head of the Department, and an advisory committee for Management and Liberal Studies was set up. In the 1961/ 1962 Annual Report the following statement appeared: 'It is the intention of the Governors to develop Management Studies at the College to the highest level'. In the next three years the College was running a sandwich course for the postgraduate Diploma of the College (DNCL) and the Diploma of the British Institute of Management (DMS). Prior to this, management was taught mainly by lecturers in the Production Engineering Department. In 1963 the new Department of Management and Social Sciences was formed; three individuals who taught management in the Production Engineering Department moved into the department, and two outsiders were brought in to help develop management education (the present author, an occupational psychologist from market research; and Douglas Vaughan, an economist from the Treasury). From 1963 the department was run as two units: 'Management Studies' and 'Social Science and Humanities'. This structural split was formalized in 1966 when the Northampton College of Advanced Technology achieved university status as City University.

The in-depth story of Cass has been described by the author in a former publication (Williams, 2006). The development of Cass in many ways mirrors the development of those business schools that grew out of the former CATs in 1966, but less so to those schools that grew out of already well-established universities (e.g. Durham, Edinburgh) or newly created universities (e.g. Warwick, Lancaster). The obvious similarity to Aston was the technological context which they shared. Two differences are equally obvious: in 1966 Aston had both undergraduate and postgraduate degrees, whereas Cass focused solely on postgraduates (reflected in the name 'Graduate Business Centre'); Aston had developed a much stronger research reputation than Cass (thanks mainly to the Industrial Administration Research Unit). It was only in 1976 that Cass recruited students to an undergraduate Business Studies degree, in recognition of which it changed its name to 'City University Business School'. As with Aston, it imported staff (and structures) from other parts of the university in order to achieve its strategic objectives. Thus, in 1982 the 'Centre for Banking and International Finance', in 1992 'Property Valuation and Management' and in 2002 'Actuarial Science and Statistics' departments merged into the business school.

Management structures evolved to accommodate growth, internal changes (e.g. academic profile) and external changes (e.g. government policies, the market). Cass progressed from informal disciplinary groups in 1966 to formal disciplinary divisions in 1977; a department (i.e. Business Studies) and three dependent centres in 1986; then two departments (i.e. Business Studies, Banking and Finance) plus Executive Education; ten departments in 1996; two Faculties in 2001 (i.e. Management, Finance) plus Executive Education; and three Faculties in 2002 (Management, Finance, Insurance and Risk Management) plus Executive Education. As one would expect the nature of these structural changes reflected strategic objectives, including: meeting the needs of the City of London (the finance faculty is considerably larger than Management); financial stability through diversification into the part-time MBA market, the specialist MSc and undergraduate markets (currently 3 MBAs, 17 MScs and 3 BScs); quality reputation through a strong research base (a low research profile in the period from 1966 to the 1980s progressed in achieving well above median ratings in RAE's of 1992 to 2008).

An interesting difference between Aston and Cass occurred with respect to their buildings. The former was based on the university campus, the latter had always aimed to be geographically closer to the financial city than its host university in Northampton Square where its traditional strength was in engineering for many years. Indeed this was the policy of the City University since the business school was seen as a key link between the University and the City. However, it was only in 2002 that the school was able to leave rented accommodation and move into its present state-of-the-art building in Bunhill Row — a 15-minute walk to the main University campus.

4.6. Management Education in Newly Created Universities

Warwick (WBS): In 1965 several new universities were created including Warwick, Lancaster and Sussex. The first two launched business schools very soon after. The source of information about WBS is mainly derived from its 40 years celebration publication (WBS, 2007). The School of Industrial and Business Studies at Warwick was established in 1967; Masters courses were launched in 1968, and the first undergraduate course in 1969. Hugh Clegg was appointed founding professor of industrial relations in 1967, and in 1970 a unit was launched that was to have a distinguished history — the Industrial Relations Research Unit. As a school on a greenfield site, WBS was able to formulate a strong mission with clear objectives; and it benefitted from the spacious grounds of its host university's campus, enabling building constructions to be planned in unison with the growth of the School. It also had the advantage of being able to appoint staff most likely to help meet its objectives. In the first year of operation WBS had 24 students, 5 staff and 3 courses; by 2007 it had 21,500 alumni, 7539 students, 304 staff (200 academic), 26 courses and a turnover of £36.5 million. At its foundation it obtained over 80% of its funding from government; now about 80% of its revenue is self-generated. This pattern is reflected in the top UK business schools generally.

In its promotional literature WBS emphasizes its aspiration to be a top business school internationally. A strong research base is one of the strategies it followed from the very beginning, and it has consistently received high ratings in the RAEs. It has also been progressive in the design of its degrees: e.g. its full-time MBA (initially labelled MSc) in 1968 was followed by an evening MBA in 1985, a distance learning MBA in 1986, and a modular study MBA in 1994. Again, these achievements are not unique to Warwick among the top schools. However, one of its features sets itself apart from others — the chairman/head was elected by colleagues until 1998. This inevitably meant that the Chair would be an academic. This practice of academic leaders continued when deans were appointed through traditional means; thus in 2000 Howard Thomas, the second Dean (as opposed to chairman) was appointed. He had previously been at LBS before holding appointments at several top American business schools. In 2000 WBS claimed to be the first UK school to be accredited by all three bodies AMBA, EQUIS and AACSB.

Lancaster University Management School (*LUMS*) shared much in common with WBS. It was founded about the same time, and its greenfield site encouraged innovative thinking. An interesting feature of its development was that each department was built around an individual known in academic circles for their contribution to knowledge in an area related to management. An example was the appointment of Sylvia Shimmin to the Chair of Behaviour in Organisations; other founding chairs were appointed in accounting, economics, operations research and marketing. Most of the top business schools have come to be associated with particular areas of knowledge as a result of one or more highly successful research centres. The example from LUMS is the Management Learning Unit, whose first research director (John Burgoyne) and colleagues have made a significant impact on the management and organizational learning literature (Pedler, Burgoyne, et al., 1991). Reference has already been made to the design of their consortium programme (Ashton & Gosling, 1991). This innovative inclination of LUMS was also exemplified in their cross-cultural MSc in Management. This was an outcome of a collaboration with Henry Mintzberg of McGill in Canada, a long-standing critic of the American MBA model for its overly academic approach (Mintzberg, 2004).

4.7. Overcoming Resistance to Change in Two Ancient Universities

The resistance of the long-established universities, as opposed to newer technological universities, to management as a respectable academic discipline is well illustrated by Cambridge. In 1954 Cambridge was offered an endowment from the Marshall Aid Fund to establish management education at the University. Lord Baker thought Cambridge should grab the money, others were much less enthusiastic. An appropriate person could not be attracted to the proposed Chair. In the end, the Engineering Department accepted the fund so that management could be taught as an option in the third year Tripos. In 1959 David Marples, a lecturer in the department, started the Principles of Industrial Management course. In 1963 Cyril Sofer (a sociologist) was recruited as a Reader to create and head a Management Studies group. A few years later Roger Mansfield was recruited as a research assistant, then as a FME Fellow — these fellowships were designed to attract academically well-qualified individuals into management education. When Stephen Watson (a mathematician) was appointed to a lectureship in operations research (also financed by the Marshall Aid Fund) he found himself part of this small management studies group. In 1971 management studies consisted of operations research, sociology and economics. 'Some engineers thought that the subject was a complete waste of time'.

In 1978 Watson became Head of the Management Studies group. As a result of UGC money to develop prestigious courses in engineering it was possible to make an appointment in IR and additional one in economics. By 1980 there were around eight lecturers in the group, and they began lobbying for a business school but realized that they needed a plan that would be acceptable to the rest of the University. An enabling factor was created when a senior partner of Peat Marwick (now KPMG) approached his *alma mater* in 1983 asking why Cambridge had no business school. As a result of the discussions that followed with Watson, a professor of management was advertised in 1984. This was the first such Chair in Oxbridge! No suitable candidate applied. In October 1986 Watson was appointed to the Chair, although he primarily regarded himself as a mathematician. This meant that in 1986 a Management Studies Tripos was introduced separate from the Engineering Tripos. Opposition to the idea of a business school was still present because it meant that the Engineering Department would have to share some of its lectureships with any new emerging structure. In order to appease some of the opposition the group followed a 'one step at a time' strategy. A review committee was established in 1988/1989, and an institute rather than a business school was duly formed — the Institute of Management Studies. An MPhil in management studies was introduced in 1990, as was a specialism in finance. An MBA was introduced in 1991 with a novel format inspired by Charles Handy; this was a three-year course designed to integrate the academic with the practical by students spending one term in each year at the University, and the rest of the time with their employer. Not surprisingly such a course was difficult for both employer and student to manage; the length was reduced to two years and eventually the more conventional one-year MBA was adopted.

In the process of searching for new accommodation for the institute an alumni of the University (together with Simon Sainsbury's Monument

Trust) came to the rescue. Paul Judge became a key benefactor having benefitted from a business school education at Wharton, after graduating in engineering at Cambridge. 'I saw the difference between British and American attitudes to management. In the UK it was seen as administration whereas in the US it was about strategy and managing change' (Judge, 2009). Sir Paul Judge wanted to help in the development of management education, accepting that it was not yet fully accepted in the UK culture. Sir Paul Judge has pointed out that these developments at Cambridge have helped to make management an acceptable subject for study. Stephen Watson left in 1994 to take up the deanship of Lancaster University Management School. Professor Sandra Dawson (now Dame) was appointed Director of the Institute in 1995; the Institute was renamed the *Judge Business School* in the same year. The new building for the School was formally opened in 1996 (the impressive redevelopment of the Old Addenbrooke's Hospital). As with other research active business schools this one has also found benefits in spearheading research through the establishment of centres, with their advantages in attracting grants, in facilitating multidisciplinary projects and in attracting publicity.

Oxford displayed the same resistance towards management (as opposed to its constituent disciplines) as a respectable academic subject as was found at Cambridge. Although the *Said Business School* was established in 1996, management education had a presence in the periphery of Oxford from 1965 when the Oxford Centre for Management Studies was founded. The Centre developed a favourable reputation for executive development courses. Rosemary Stewart, a member of its staff from the early years, had already made an impact on management education more generally through various well-read publications. John Child has pointed out that relatively little had been published on the relevance of the findings of the social sciences to management before the appearance of her book 'The Reality of Management' (Stewart, 1963). In its early days the Centre was an 'associate institution' of the University, mainly providing executive courses but then extending to undergraduate and postgraduate degrees. In 1983 it was renamed Templeton College and in 1991 the University of Oxford School of Management Studies was created, taking over the degree courses. Said School grew out of the latter following a £23 million benefaction from the Syrian businessman Wafic Said. When this gift was made public it aroused some opposition because Said's fortune was partly accumulated through defence contracts between United Kingdom and Saudi Arabia; this explained why the opening of the impressive new building for the School in 2001 was accompanied by student protests. Since 2005 Said Business School has also taken over the running of the University's business executive education programme, formerly run by Templeton College. Said school is now rated highly in the *FT* rankings.

4.8.   Undergraduate Management Education

So far we have focused on business schools based in institutions that were universities by 1966. A large category of colleges became involved in degree-level management education in the early 1960s as a result of the Crick Report (Crick, 1964). These colleges entered the field through under-graduate courses, and their degrees were accredited by the newly formed CNAA. Of these colleges, 35 had the status of 'polytechnic' before becoming universities when the 1992 Further and Higher Education Act came into force; an additional 29 colleges were given university status in 1992. For illustrative purposes, case studies of two of these institutions are given below. However, these cases do not convey the scope of the contribution of post-1992 universities to business and management education in the United Kingdom. This will be partly rectified by Box 4.2. It lists those academic institutions in CNAA's 1989–1990 directory for first degree and under-graduate courses in Business Studies. Alongside each entry are the name of the college/polytechnic in 1990, the current university name and the title of its business or management school as it appears in the ABS list of members.

It will be recalled that in Chapter 2 attention was drawn to those institutions whose management education courses were accredited by CNAA. In parallel with the university-based institutions they formed their own association (i.e. AMEC in the 1970s, renamed AMBE in 1987). In the early days the CNAA accredited institutions focused on undergraduate programmes, while the university-based institutions were primarily con-cerned with postgraduate programmes. This differentiating feature has gradually been eroded, and a more unified management education scene has emerged as reflected by the formation of ABS in 1992.

The following information on the development of *Kingston Business School* is based largely on a paper by Professor David Miles (1996), and his observations on 10 years as Dean of the School (1986–1996). Many of the technical colleges, of which Kingston was one, had been involved in management education before 1963; but it was not until the CNAA was established in 1964 that accreditation in degree-level courses in business studies began.

The boundaries of accepted practice were narrow and the range of permitted experimentation limited. In 1967 the CNAA Business Studies Board considered eleven courses and rejected seven. The result was a similar formula of course throughout the country operating in all thirty polytechnics and a substantial number of other colleges. The number of validated courses grew from 4 in 1965, to 37 in 1974, to 146 in 1991.

Box 4.2. Institutions appearing in CNAA's 1989–1990 directory for first degree and undergraduate courses in Business Studies.

- Anglia Higher Education College: Anglia Ruskin University: Ashcroft International Business School
- Birmingham Polytechnic: Birmingham City University: Birmingham City Business School
- Bolton Institute of Higher Education: University of Bolton: Bolton Business School
- Brighton Polytechnic: University of Brighton: Brighton Business School
- Bristol Polytechnic: University of West of England: Bristol Business School
- Buckinghamshire College of Higher Education: University of Buckingham: University of Buckingham Business School
- City of London Polytechnic: London Metropolitan University: London Metropolitan Business School
- South Bank Polytechnic: University of Greenwich: University of Greenwich Business School
- Coventry Polytechnic: Coventry University: Coventry Business School
- Dorset Institute of Higher Education: Bournemouth University: Bournemouth University Business School
- Dundee Institute of Technology: University of Abertay Dundee: Dundee Business School
- Ealing College of Higher Education: Thames Valley University: Thames Valley University Business School
- Glasgow College: Glasgow Caledonian University: Caledonian Business School
- Hatfield College: University of Hertfordshire: University of Hertfordshire Business School
- Humberside College of Higher Education: University of Lincolnshire and Humberside: Lincoln Business School
- Kingston Polytechnic: Kingston University: Kingston Business School
- Lancashire Polytechnic: University of Central Lancashire: Lancashire Business School
- Leeds Polytechnic: Leeds Metropolitan University: Leeds Business School
- Leicester Polytechnic: De Montfort University: Leeds Business School
- The Liverpool Polytechnic: Liverpool John Moores University: Liverpool University Business School
- Luton College of Higher Education: University of Bedfordshire: University of Bedfordshire Business School
- Manchester Polytechnic: The Metropolitan University of Manchester: Manchester Metropolitan University Business School
- Middlesex Polytechnic: University of Middlesex: Middlesex University Business School

- Napier Polytechnic Edinburgh: Edinburgh Napier University: Edinburgh Napier Business School
- Newcastle upon Tyne Polytechnic: Northumbria University: Newcastle Business School
- Nottingham Polytechnic: Nottingham Trent University: Nottingham Business School
- Oxford Polytechnic: Oxford Brookes University: Oxford Brookes University Business School
- Paisley College of Technology: University of West of Scotland: University of West of Scotland Business School
- The Polytechnic of Central London: University of Westminster: Westminster Business School
- Polytechnic of East London: University of East London: Royal Docks Business School
- Polytechnic of Huddersfield: University of Huddersfield: University of Huddersfield Business School
- The Polytechnic of North London: London Metropolitan University: London Metropolitan Business School
- Polytechnic of South West: University of Plymouth: Plymouth Business School
- The Polytechnic of South Wales: University of Glamorgan: Glamorgan Business School
- Portsmouth Polytechnic: University of Portsmouth: Portsmouth Business School
- Robert Gordon's Institute of Technology: Robert Gordon University: Aberdeen Business School
- Salford College of Technology: University of Salford: Salford University Business School
- Sheffield City Polytechnic: Sheffield Hallam University: Sheffield Business School
- Southampton Institute of Higher Education: Southampton Solent University: Southampton Business School
- Staffordshire Polytechnic: Staffordshire University: Staffordshire University Business School
- Sunderland Polytechnic: University of Sunderland: Sunderland Business School
- Teesside Polytechnic: University of Teesside: Teesside Business School
- Thames Polytechnic: Thames Valley University: Thames Valley University Business School
- West Glamorgan Institute of Higher Education: Swansea Metropolitan University: Swansea Business School
- Wolverhampton Polytechnic: University of Wolverhampton: University of Wolverhampton Business School

The BA Business Studies core comprised: a four year course including a one year placement in industry; a period typically of two years in which foundation disciplines were studied — economics, mathematics, statistics, sociology, psychology, law, politics, accountancy; an opportunity to specialize in one of the principal business functions — marketing, manufacture, finance, and personnel. The courses needed to demonstrate explicitly that the intellectual attainment matched that of more conventional degrees. Business students needed to show graduate qualities: the ability to learn independently; to understand that facts have a limited reality without the illumination of theory; to understand the nature of evidence and to have a proper respect for it; to have the ability to concentrate over prolonged periods of time, to produce reflected assessments, to present well argued solutions to problems, and to write clearly and concisely. The ability to conceive information in quantitative terms, manipulate it, deduce consequences and induce explanations. Another consistent theme of CNAA was the need to demonstrate the integration of knowledge and technique drawn from individual disciplines ... ... The consistency of approach enabled the label 'BA Business Studies' to be widely understood among parents and schools and it rapidly became one of the most popular degree programmes in the UK. CNAA enrolment statistics demonstrate the scale of growth over the period. 129 students were enrolled in 1965, a figure which grew to over 30,000 by 1991 (Miles, 1996).

The DMS was offered at Kingston from the early 1960s, and Miles points out that for much of the time over 100 managers a year have qualified. Kingston Polytechnic was designated in 1970 by the Secretary of State for Education (Margaret Thatcher) as a Regional Management Centre for London and the South East. The idea behind the centres was to create sufficient critical mass of resources so that the constituent colleges would be able to achieve and maintain the desired standard for their qualifications. A number of progressive developments took place during the 1980s. An open learning version of the DMS was launched in 1988 in partnership with the Rapid Results College; this soon became an in-house product. In the same year a partnership was established with BPP (a private company) to deliver an MBA through open learning. When BPP withdrew from the arrangement, Kingston took on the ownership of the course. These incidents of sharing know-how and materials enabled Kingston to develop successful open learning courses with the minimal risk and resources.

Other key developments at Kingston were the introduction of an MBA in 1984, and the formation of its Business School in 1985. The latter involved combining the resources of the Schools of Management Education and Business together with a substantial group of lecturers from the School of Economics and Politics and the School of Sociology. Some of the disadvantages of a structure built on discipline groups were mitigated by the School occupying a new building with strong technical resources. In addition to the 'general' MBA degree, a number of specialist MScs have been launched in support of professional careers in functional areas such as marketing, finance, personnel management.

Aberdeen Business School had similar technological backgrounds as Aston and Cass. Detailed information relating to it can be found in Gourlay's account (Gourlay, 2005). Management made its first appearance in 1945 in a series of training courses for ex-officers in the university's antecedent institution — Robert Gordon's Technical College. From 1953 courses were run which enabled students to gain the Intermediate Certificate in Management Studies. It was in 1963 that the Department of Business Studies had its first intake of students for the nationally recognized DMS. Prior to that date management studies had made an uncertain start; it was based successively in the School of Architecture and then in the School of Engineering, and then linked with liberal studies. Problems were encountered in finding accommodation and in recruiting academic staff, and only in October 1965 was a head of department appointed. A few months before that the College was renamed Robert Gordon's Institute of Technology (RGIT). 1965 is identified as the year in which Aberdeen Business School was founded: a head was appointed (Joseph Batty); it had its own premises; a three-year full-time diploma in commerce plus part-time courses in management were offered.

In 1966 some of the Head's plans were blocked by the Scottish Education Department. They did not want RGIT to establish a CNAA degree in business studies because the competition would have adverse consequences for Dundee Institute of Technology, who were expecting to introduce such a degree in 1968. One of the outcomes was to encourage Aberdeen to develop postgraduate courses before its proposed undergraduate degree. Thus, the full-time course preparing students for graduateship of the IPM was extended to include a spell of full-time experience in a personnel department, thereby qualifying for a RGIT diploma in addition to any success in the IPM external examinations. By 1970 the rationalization attempted by the Scottish Education Department in the tertiary education sector meant that RGIT was selected as one to concentrate on degree and postgraduate degree and diploma work. This enabled the BA in Business Studies (validated by the CNAA) to be launched, and approval was also obtained from the CNAA for its two previous postgraduate degrees.

In 1969/1970 the new Head, Ralph Hart, raised the question of research. This was premature since nothing in the public funds was allocated to colleges/polytechnics for research, even though the CNAA expected research to be carried out in those institutions it validated. The other problem at the end of the 1970s was accommodation, 'hopelessly inadequate for the needs of a business school' particularly one 'recruiting so many students of high calibre to courses which reflected the demands of industry and commerce'. A move to a purpose-built accommodation was delayed for various reasons including finance, but new premises eventually were ready in 1998/1999. In 1989 a part-time MBA was launched as a joint degree with the University of Aberdeen. In 1992 degree-granting status was conferred on RGIT and it took on the new title of The Robert Gordon University, and both institutions found themselves competing for students. The new head realized that a higher profile was needed and he implemented a strategy to achieve this, including: registering the name 'Aberdeen Business School' (not used until four years later after major restructuring of the University); focusing particularly on the oil industry and oil-related businesses. The establishment of the Business Research Unit attracted research/consultancy funds from the oil industry and research students from overseas. In 1998 it established an Open Learning Unit to provide distance learning materials, and this enabled it to obtain several corporate training contracts. A BA in European Business Administration with languages had been launched towards the end of the 1980s, and this proved a useful contributor in the development of an international orientation and in the development of new learning methods. The school has established mutually useful contacts with several countries, including Kazakhstan and China; and has formed partnerships with institutions in seven European countries. Through its e-learning system the university can deliver courses all around the world, and has become an international player in university education. For example, in 2005 it became the first university in the United Kingdom to be approved to deliver an online Chartered Institute of Personnel and Development course.

4.9. Other Selected Histories

There remain a large number of other business schools whose history could have been covered. A few of these are included here because they appear to add something different to the overall picture. *Cranfield School of Management* was founded in 1967. It has consistently performed well in the *FT* rankings (see Tables 4.1–4.3). Its parent university had a similar technological background to Aston and Cass. Two features set itself apart from other top schools in the United Kingdom: it is a postgraduate institution (as LBS); it has developed a strong reputation for teaching. The result is that the average age of its MBA students is somewhat higher than its competitors, and it places special emphasis on the personal professional development of the participants. As with other top schools it has formed strategic alliances with several schools around the world.

So far no business school based in Wales has been mentioned. The development of *Cardiff Business School* (*CBS*) has an interesting history (Mansfield, 2010). It is an example of two embryonic business schools coming together as a result of the merger of two parent institutions in higher education — i.e. the University of Wales Institute of Science and Technology (UWIST) and University College, Cardiff (UCC). UWIST originated from an institution created in 1866, focusing on technical matters. Within a year it began teaching commerce, and in 1896 the Commercial Department was one of four which later formed the Cardiff Technical College. As with several other technical colleges in the United Kingdom it gradually ejected its lower level courses. Its first university level qualification was an external degree of the University of London — the BSc (Econ). In 1953 it became known as the College of Technology and Commerce and in 1957 it achieved the status of a CAT (one of eight in the United Kingdom). Following the Robbins Report it gained university status as UWIST in 1968. A significant component of the future CBS was the Department of Business and Social Studies; this became two departments in the 1970s — Applied Economics, and Business Administration and Accountancy. Before the split the former component gained the Sir Julian Hodge Chair in Banking and Finance, and soon after the latter gained the Sir Julian Hodge Chair in Accountancy. These two endowed Chairs marked a significant turning point in the development of business-related subjects, and in 1976 Roger Mansfield was appointed Professor of Business Administration. The precursor to the MBA in the 1980s was the MSc in Management and Technology which was launched in 1971. This latter degree was based in the newly created Centre for Graduate Management Studies — an inter-departmental structure. In an effort to improve inter-departmental co-operation the two departments above were merged in 1985 as the Department of Business and Economics, and the Centre for Graduate Management Studies was renamed the Cardiff Business School.

The second university that merged in 1988 was UCC, founded in 1883 as the University College of South Wales and Monmouthshire (one of three university colleges to form the University of Wales in 1893). From the point of view of CBS, the relevant department here was that of Political and Commercial Science which was changed to Economics and Political Science in 1910. In 1930 the Montague Burton Chair in Industrial Relations was established leading to the creation of the Department of Industrial Relations and Management Studies. Accountancy was first introduced in 1946. 'The professional accountancy bodies had decided that the recruitment of graduates to the profession should be encouraged and had opened discussions with representatives of 10 universities, including Cardiff, in order to discuss how far the universities could accommodate the needs of students who would read for a degree which included economics, accountancy and law in roughly equal proportions. The Faculty of Arts in University College Cardiff accepted proposals which met this requirement and the provision of appropriate courses in accountancy became the responsibility of the Department of Economics' (Mansfield, 2010). In 1973 a separate Department of Accountancy and Financial Control was established; about the same time law and politics also achieved independence from Economics. A major but slow development in the 1960s was the partial separation of management from industrial relations. This was facilitated by funding for additional staff from FME.

Formal discussions for merging the two universities took place between 1981 and 1987, but decisive action only occurred as a result of the financial difficulties of UCC. 'The University Grants Committee was no longer prepared to continue to pay grant to University College unless certain conditions were met. In essence the requirement was an immediate irrevocable commitment to merge from both University College and UWIST. Subject to that and the establishment of an Executive Commission with authority over both institutions, an interest free loan was arranged and grant continued to be paid. This Executive Commission was established in July 1987 and, as one of its first acts, decided that the immediate merger of activities relating to business and also relating to law should take place prior to the formal merger of the two institutions. ... Thus the staff of the Departments of Accountancy and Financial Control, Economics, and Industrial Relations and Management Studies of University College were seconded to UWIST to join with the staff of the Department of Business and Economics at UWIST to become the Cardiff Business School' (Mansfield, 2010). In November 1987 the newly created business school was inaugurated by Prince Charles, Chancellor of the University of Wales. In the following year the major components of the School were located in the same building. There were four sub-units in the management structure: Accounting and Finance; Economics; Human Resource Management; Marketing and Strategy.

Some further observations made by Roger Mansfield are relevant: there was strong support from the top (i.e. the Principal of UWIST was also Principal of the merged institutions; and the Deputy Principal of UWIST was Mansfield himself during the critical formation of CBS); the main opposition to developments came from the economists in both institutions; the School's strategy was to be strong academically, and this meant that limited resources were devoted to post-experience education, and admission to the MBA programme was largely based on academic merit not work experience.

The *Open Business School* also has an interesting story to tell. In 1983 Derek Pugh left LBS to join the systems group in the faculty of technology at the Open University. He soon was arguing for the establishment of a business school, and in 1988 one was established in the Faculty of Management. Professor Andrew Thomson, Dean of the Business School at Glasgow University, was appointed to head it and he was quick to invite Pugh to transfer from the Faculty of Technology and to join him in the business school. From the start the School focused on short courses for practising managers. Since 1982 a very successful module 'The Effective Manager' had been offered to students. The module was the work of a team led by Charles Handy. As part of plans to enter the postgraduate market, exploratory talks for some sort of linkage were held with Henley and Ashridge; but these came to nothing. One of Thomson's main goals was to set up an MBA programme; a key factor enabling this to come about was a grant of £400,000 from the DES. The first MBA students were enrolled in 1989.

The uniqueness of the Open University, which recruited its first students in 1971, is that they have a very open admissions policy and their programmes are based on distance learning technology. Geographical location was no barrier to learning at the Open University, and therefore an early strategy of the business school was to extend their courses across Europe, and subsequently worldwide. In terms of student numbers the Open Business School is by far the largest in the United Kingdom. Although weak on research it has shown itself to be strong on quality of teaching, accessibility, flexibility and international orientation.

Before moving down to Milton Keynes to head the Open Business School, Andrew Thomson was Dean at Glasgow from 1983. Prior to that there was a move to form a *Scottish Business School*, based on the relevant units in Glasgow, Strathclyde and Edinburgh Universities. The driving force for this proposed structure came from CIME who provided the money. The group was subsequently widened to include others, e.g. Dundee and Robert Gordon. Apart from a part-time MBA and a PhD programme started by David Buchanan, there was little co-operation on the part of the constituent parts of the Scottish Business School. Besides the original common source of finance there was no rationale for them to form a coherent body — each thought they were better than the others and competed against each other. The concept of a Scottish Business School proved largely unsuccessful.

Hull University started life in 1927 as a College of the University of London, and it was not until 1954 that it obtained its Royal Charter and was thus able to award its own degrees. The main source of information for its history is based on a document sent to ABS in response to a request (Hull, 2009). Economics and commerce were founding subjects in 1927, but Hull University Business School (HUBS) was not established until 1999 when the schools of accounting, business and finance, and management were merged.

Its early guiding vision was 'to become a full-service business school that is recognized internationally as a leading UK business school', and its mission to be 'a customer-focused, full-service business school contributing to the development of international business excellence and serving its regions'. Compared to some of the other schools discussed above, HUBS is a young school. But being based on existing departments, and being joined by others (e.g. Department of Economics became part of the school in 2002) it has rapidly grown in size and strength within the University. It shares similar strategic objectives with other university-based business schools in the United Kingdom; and thus its achievements reflect those pursued by its competitors with respect to superior performance in QAA and RAE assessments, stamp of approval from AMBA and EQUIS, world-class premises and facilities, introducing structures to enhance links with local businesses. In relation to the latter, the University of Hull Logistics Institute was established in 2005 in a project led by the business school, attracting 'significant grants from the Regional Development Agency and the European Regional Development Fund to enable the institute to provide research-led consultancy, training, and education relevant to the commercial ports and logistics sector that is a key part of the local and regional economy'. In 2008 the institute was fully integrated into the school while retaining its commercial focus.

St Andrews School of Management is an example of another 'young' business school, but this time located in one of the most ancient universities in the United Kingdom (third oldest in the English-speaking world). The early start of the School is described by Peter McKiernan: 'The School was formed in 2004 as a result of a merger between the University's traditional Department of Management, specializing in undergraduate and doctoral degrees, and the recently constructed Centre for Business Education, specialising in taught Masters degrees. The Department was formed in 1987, from its base as a youthful sub unit within the long-established, Department of Economics. The University strategic plan had identified the 3 Ms of Management, Media and Medicine, as growth areas over the forthcoming years and so support was strong and enduring. This was counter cultural, as the ancient and traditional university context tended to privilege the well-established Arts, Humanities and Sciences rather than develop new domains' (personal communication).

The School thrived despite the internal cultural clashes that occurred during the first three years. The interesting observation to make about this School was its strategic decision to build on its traditional strengths; this meant deliberately avoiding the MBA market and focusing on taught Masters degrees (e.g. Finance and Management; Management and Information Technology; Human Resource Management; Research — Management Studies). Nine of these were developed in the first five years and each was filled to capacity. In 2008 the School was accredited by the Central and Eastern European Management Development Association (CEEMAN), and it is in the process of seeking accreditations from EQUIS and AACSB. The School sees itself developing as a top 'boutique' international business school.

Roffey Park Management College is an independent institution involved in management education; it was founded as a charitable trust in 1946 (in the 1970s it replaced 'centre' with 'college' in its name), and celebrated its 60 years in 2006 (RoffeyPark, 2006). Its history has similarities with Henley and Ashridge in that its focus has primarily been on executive development courses, although its early activities were short residential courses on the socio-medical problems of industry. In 1957 it ran its first corporate programme — a series of short courses for all levels of British European Airways management. Roffey Park's strength was in human aspects of management, both in the context of research and training. In 1967 it became a limited company and a registered charity. In the 1980s it became more involved in research on projects with the University of Sussex, particularly on cross-cultural research into management. It publishes research reports which are designed to make an input into its courses (e.g. 'Managing teams across cultures'; 'Strategic alliances: Getting the people bit right'). In 1989 it introduced an innovative MBA by self-managed learning, within the context of self-evaluated learning sets of 5–7 people each with a specially trained Set Adviser. Students were all practicing managers, and they each identified a major project as a vehicle. The learning process required each student to understand in depth the projects of their fellow set members. The last students graduated in 2003. Although the course was accredited by the University of Sussex, its failure to meet the accreditation criteria of AMBA created difficulties for marketing the course. Val Hammond (Director of Roffey Park at that time) points out 'Nevertheless, our graduates have gone on to distinguish themselves as directors, managing directors, Vice-Presidents and CEOs in companies and public bodies in this country and around the world' (personal communication).

Roffey Park also introduced an MSc in Management Development in 1990, accredited by Salford University. This continues to run successfully under the new title of MSc in People and Organisational Development, which is now accredited by Sussex University. The year 2003 saw the opening of improved conference and accommodation facilities at Roffey Park.

4.10. Observations Relating to the Case Studies

Although the above case studies are not intended to be a scientific sample of 'business schools' in the United Kingdom, they do include several schools that have consistently shown themselves to be in the 'top category' as defined by the *FT* rankings. Some schools have been added in the expectation that greater diversity may yield further insights into the development of business schools in the United Kingdom. Observations worth noting include:

- The pre-eminent position of LBS. Originally one of the two financially favoured business schools which were intended to be seen in the same category as the top American schools such as Harvard and Wharton. LBS followed closely the American model in terms of the length of the MBA degree, its research orientation, paying the international rate for top academics etc. In the *FT* rankings for 2010 the full-time LBS MBA is ranked number one in the world; thus fulfilling the original expectations of the Franks Report.
- The other financially favoured school, MBS, has experienced more turbulent times. It tried to develop and implement its own philosophy of management education. The 'experiment' had adverse effects on its research performance, and it failed to negotiate the degree of autonomy that LBS had from London University. One could argue that its 'leadership' was found wanting at various times in the past. Now its future looks a lot more promising as a result of the merger of 2004. This precedent of the merger of the parent institutions of business schools may turn out to be one way of enabling business schools to survive the global competition in management education.
- Many of the former CATs gaining university status in 1966 have found their way in the top 100 of the *FT* rankings. Although some of their strategies may have differed from each other, they appear to have taken advantage of their inherent or potential strengths by aligning strategy to local opportunities; e.g. Cass to the financial industry, Aberdeen to the oil industry.
- Other schools not necessarily blessed with obvious opportunities have concentrated in building a unique brand image that has proved beneficial, e.g. Cranfield's reputation for teaching.
- Many schools have developed strategies that utilize the strengths or know-how of their parent universities, such as the Open Business School.
- Two schools were latecomers to the management education scene (i.e. Judge and Said) but the international image and support of their parent universities soon ensured that they moved up the rankings.
- Schools that emerged from earlier technical colleges and polytechnics (with their engineering context) were less inhibited in developing business and management qualifications (e.g. Aston, Kingston) than those emerging from traditional universities (e.g. Oxford and Cambridge). This applies to most of the institutions belonging to the post-1992 universities; probably brought about by their close ties with the community and the

training needs of the local industry (e.g. Glamorgan, Birmingham City University, Anglia Ruskin).

- Business schools are multidisciplinary structures catering for a variety of markets, e.g. undergraduates and postgraduates, entrepreneurs and corporations, profit-making and not-for-profit organizations etc. It is therefore not surprising to find that schools have developed strengths in some areas and not others, and that their development has involved many structural changes. These structural changes may be part of the process of formally creating a school with the resources to succeed in a competitive environment (e.g. CBS); or of strengthening an existing school by drawing in academic resources belonging to other parts of the parent institution (e.g. Actuarial Science and Statistics merged into Cass Business School). Some schools have even eschewed the idea of developing an MBA programme in favour of focusing resources on specialist management degrees, and thereby quickly developing a brand that differentiates them from the highly competitive MBA market (e.g. St Andrews School of Management).

- As part of the processes of formation and/or adaptation, all schools have experienced obstacles to change (e.g. restructuring to increase greater co-operation between sub-units). Resistance to change is mainly a consequence of the compartmentalization of disciplines combined with the 'departmental' structure for managing universities. This is where the leadership of those with the power to influence things by managing the boundaries is so important. Examples can be found in all schools.

- Those who have not managed to sustain themselves as financially stable and independent schools, have resorted to merging with other stronger institutions in receipt of public funds, e.g. Henley merging with Reading University.

- Business schools can no longer ignore the presence of accrediting bodies (e.g. AMBA) recognized as successfully setting quality standards. For example, failure to meet their criteria for an MBA will adversely affect recruitment; in time such programmes will be terminated despite their merits (e.g. Roffey Park's MBA). Achieving the accreditation stamp of the three most status giving bodies (i.e. AMBA, EQUIS, AACSB) is the strategic goal of a number of schools and several in the United Kingdom have now achieved this distinction (e.g. Aston, Cass, Warwick).

While there are similarities in the historical development of UK business schools, the disparities are equally striking. These patterns are almost certainly determined by common environmental factors (e.g. Funding Councils, accrediting bodies) interacting with unique environmental and institutional factors (e.g. local businesses, leadership and organizational culture).

Chapter 5

Conclusions: The Historical Development of UK Management Education

In reviewing the subject matter covered in this book, an observation that comes immediately to mind is that business and management education in the United Kingdom readily falls into two halves — the 'gestation' phase prior to the 1960s, and the 'business school' phase from then to the present day. The gestation phase is characterized by the leadership of a number of pioneering individuals (e.g. Lyndall Urwick), and a number of tentative academic interventions in management education. The latter included those universities offering degrees and diplomas in commerce with some elements of management. The early 1930s also saw Sir Montagu Burton endowing chairs in industrial relations at three universities. An American observer to the British scene points out 'The total enrolment in university courses in business administration in the US in 1930 was eighty times that in Great Britain. Since 1930 the disparity has increased. ... It was not until 1936 that Great Britain had a national body eligible for membership in the International Committee for Scientific Management. During his presidency of this committee, Lord Leverhume in that year succeeded in establishing a British Management Council to serve as a coordinating body of the numerous groups concerned with the management movement' (Murphy, 1953, p. 39). This council was eventually replaced by the BIM in 1948 with initial finance from the government. In the 1940s and 1950s it was more the technical colleges and polytechnics that took up management education and training rather than the universities.

The expansion of management education in the 'business school' phase (i.e. 1960s to the present) has been impressive to say the least. Note the findings in Chapter 4.

5.1.   A Dynamic Model to Synthesize Findings

The emergence and consolidation of a 'business school industry' has been brought about by a complex mix of factors. It is this mix that the remainder of this section will attempt to conceptualize through an interconnected framework or model. One of the most enduring paradigms in the organizational behaviour literature is that of Kurt Lewin — his force-field theory in which equilibrium is achieved in a dynamic system by forces for change confronting forces against change (Lewin, 1951). This force-field analogy has been used by others in helping to understand the historical developments of management education (Wilson & Thomson, 2006). An ally of the status quo is 'culture', a concept used to refer to relatively stable sets of beliefs of social groups and to the traditional ways of getting things done in a social system. It is now self-evident that organizational entities (e.g. nation, firm, business school) are continually coping with changes in their environment. A wide range of coping mechanisms is available. For example: they can develop new products to service new markets; they can merge with others in order to survive financial crises; and they can educate their human resources to utilize new knowledge for selecting and managing their strategies for developing effective coping responses. These processes have been ongoing throughout the years covered by this history (and indeed throughout history!). The significant difference now is that thanks to more scientific mind-sets, the resulting accumulation of knowledge, and the institutionalization of 'good' practice, formal management education has become part of accepted practice and therefore embedded itself in the culture of the United Kingdom. The 'business school' coping response is very visible in advanced economies, and is spreading to developing economies. The establishment of bodies corresponding to ABS in these countries is evidence of this trend. The fact that this publication is focusing solely on the United Kingdom is not intended to indicate that developments on the international front were less important or did not have significance for the UK scene. Other publications present a European or international perspective (e.g. Antunes & Thomas, 2007).

Historical developments in management education in the United Kingdom have been the theme of this book. Figure 0.1 presented a simple model to guide one through an overwhelming mass of information. Figure 5.1 is an attempt to provide a framework that brings together the many elements identified and explored in researching the theme. This 'model' in effect analyses and elaborates the element in Figure 0.1 labelled *Forces underlying developments in management education*. The labels used in the model incorporate in a condensed form the list of milestones identified previously (see Box 1.2). While 'leaders' and 'leadership' have been used throughout the

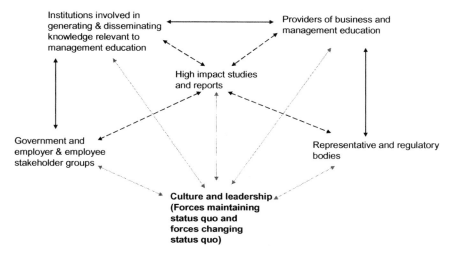

Fig. 5.1: A dynamic model to account for the historical development of
management education in the United Kingdom.

text they have intentionally not been defined so far. *Leadership* is used to
describe the behaviours/actions of a single individual or group, or institution.
Acts of leadership refer to those behaviours/actions which initiate, support
and manage coping responses in the face of environmental challenges. It
follows from this operational definition that a host of individuals mentioned
in earlier sections have displayed leadership behaviours that have had a
positive impact on the development of management education in the United
Kingdom. They include industrialists (e.g. Seebohm Rowntree), consultants
(e.g. Lyndall Urwick), public servants (e.g. Lord Franks), Chairs of
representative/regulatory bodies (e.g. Sir George Bain at CUMS), Chairs of
learned societies (e.g. Professor Cary Cooper at BAM), Deans of business
schools (e.g. Dr. Arthur Earle at LBS), influential academics (e.g. Charles
Handy) etc. But their influence in facilitating change has only been possible
because they formally represented, or informally reflected, a network
of other supportive individuals or institutions. This is shown diagrammati-
cally in Figure 5.1. *Culture and leadership* share the same space in the
model, because the leadership process involves changing and reinforcing
aspects of culture. In other words, the leadership process influences the forces
likely to maintain and/or change the *status quo*. This understanding of
leadership and organizational culture owes much to the work of Edgar Schein
(1985), and has been further explored elsewhere by the present author
(Williams, 2001).

High impact studies and reports appear throughout the list of milestones in Box 1.2. Distinctive features of these reports that account for their subsequent impact, include:

(i)   ʰeir preparation those stakeholders who have a direct interest in the outcomes would have been consulted (e.g. government and employer stakeholders).
(2) The nominal leader (e.g. Chairman) was a well respected and credible business person or academic (e.g. Sir Charles Baillieu in 1945, Sir George Bain in 1994).
(3) The sponsors were powerful institutions, often with direct representation on the team or committee overseeing the study (e.g. FBI, FME).

The Urwick Report in 1947, the Crick Report in 1964 and the Constable/McCormick Report 1987 all shared these features. The Franks Report was slightly different in that Lord Franks was selected to carry out the study by two opposing groups of businessmen — those supporting the idea of business schools attached to universities versus those who were very much against this proposal (the 'Savoy Group').

Representative and regulatory bodies covers those stakeholder groups described in Chapter 2 as having a direct interest in management education, particularly in management departments and business schools (e.g. CNAA, ABS, AMBA). This element includes the professional bodies associated with management and involved in setting standards and criteria for membership for general and specialist managers (e.g. Chartered Institute of Management, Chartered Institute of Personnel and Development). *Institutions involved in generating and disseminating knowledge relevant to management education* included those learned societies and research councils who play a part in initiating and monitoring the quality of knowledge associated with management education through their sponsorships, grant making and publishing activities (e.g. FME, BAM, ESRC).

Government, employer and employee stakeholder groups includes government departments and agencies (e.g. DES, HEFCE), employer bodies (e.g. Confederation of British Industry) and employee bodies (e.g. Unions).

Providers of business and management education focuses on one of the two common elements in Figures 0.1 and 5.1. The providers identified have included academia, consultancies and corporations themselves. However, attention has been on academia since this is where the main thrust has emerged. Individuals with experience of American business schools, either as students or visitors, were impressed with what they saw across the Atlantic. Some of these have been referred to above, and one may add politicians to this list as well (e.g. Sir Keith Joseph). The attractiveness of the business school model stemmed from a mix of factors: the perceived association between American productivity and its business schools; the post-war uncompetitiveness of the British economy; the growth of knowledge directly relevant to the role of manager, and the strengthening belief that the training and education of managers would yield valuable outcomes; the beliefs that recruits from academia (particularly universities as opposed to technical colleges) would attract superior talent into British industry; the first-hand experience of senior industrialists to formal management education at Henley Staff College and elsewhere. These and other factors, including the report of Lord Franks in 1963 and the already successful forages of polytechnics and colleges of technology in management education, all combined to bring about the creation of business schools as one of the most effective coping responses the country could make to environmental challenges.

5.2. The Role of Leadership

As indicated in the case studies, the early business schools were not guaranteed a smooth sailing pathway. They required effective leadership to survive the unpredictability of State income, to avoid the excesses of the 'cash cow' syndrome of parent universities towards their business schools, to tackle the proliferation of competing schools at home and abroad, to deal with criticisms from employers, the government and even students. As this research has shown the coping responses of leaders (senior faculty) in schools proved successful by:

- Recruiting powerful supporters in business and among alumni.
- Creating structures for institutionalizing, regulating and promoting quality improvement in the business school industry.
- Ensuring the maintenance of high standards for student learning experiences.
- Creating courses and experiences that will help students achieve their career aspirations.
- Improving the quality of research relevant to business and management.
- Developing clear strategies aligned to their strengths, and recognizing the significance of potential contextual factors (political, economic, social and technology) (Thomas, 2007).
- Initiating or supporting internal institutional restructuring in the interest of strategic objectives and, in rare cases, mergers with external bodies.
- Developing strong relationships with alumni and institutional friends, several of whom helped to finance new buildings (e.g. Sir Paul Judge at Cambridge) and new academic developments (e.g. Peter Cullum of Towergate Partnership financing a centre for entrepreneurship at Cass).

- Drawing on the expertise of professionals in finance, HRM, operations and marketing in the process of managing business schools (the influence of 'administrators' is controversial but has the backing of governments in the interest of greater efficiency).

The above partly explains why the *Culture and leadership* element is given in boldface in the model. This element feeds from, and feeds into, all the other elements; hence the dynamic nature of the model. In the first gestation phase of management education in the UK (i.e. prior to the 1960s) leadership on the part of industrialists, government departments and professional associations was critical. As the business school phase or 'industry' unfolded, it acquired more power and influence; deans could now negotiate with their parent universities in ways which were not possible 20 years or so earlier. This has brought more responsibility to business schools *vis-à-vis* their local and international communities; particularly in ensuring that the educational needs of their client students and corporations are met, and that relevant knowledge is available for coping with new environmental challenges.

The 'UK National Forum for Employers and Business School Deans' was formed in 2003 by the Council for Industry and Higher Education and ABS to facilitate better understanding between the parties, and to increase the mutual benefits from this relationship. The Forum was one of several initiatives arising from the CEML Report (CEML, 2002b) to improve the United Kingdom's competitiveness through skills development and enhanced learning capabilities. The six meetings of the Forum over two years fulfilled original intentions in terms of time, but output expectations were only partially met. To quote the final report:

> Whilst input from the business world, including from forum members, has been possible and valuable when made, it remains a feature of the dialogue between business schools and business that too few CEOs from business saw merit in attending the forum. This has impacted on the original vision that the forum should comprise a small but sufficient number of deans and CEOs, supported but not supplanted by other interested stakeholders. This sheds interesting light on the differing demands, motivations and needs placed on deans and CEOs. It may reflect a trend on the part of businesses to devolve personal development more to individuals. Hence building stronger relations between the HR departments of businesses and business schools may be a way to take forward the output of the forum. A direct consequence of this is some imbalance in the evidence in this report from the demand side

of business compared with the data available from the supply side (CIME & ABS, 2006).

It is possible that the apparent disinterest of CEOs in structures such as the Forum is because management and business education is now in a 'mature phase' where their direct intervention is no longer required as it was in the 'crisis conditions' of the 1940s, 1950s and 1960s. Prior to the Second World War only a handful of outstanding industrialists (e.g. Seebohm Rowntree) had nourished the 'gestation phase' in the United Kingdom. The three decades following the War were in marked contrast, as industrialists were prepared to take the lead and academia began to respond more positively.

An ever-present dilemma in management education has been the 'rigour versus relevance' controversy; a dilemma largely resolved by the professional schools of law and medicine. Since this reflects the strongly held beliefs of different stakeholders (i.e. academics versus business people) the balance between the two will fluctuate according to situational factors. Fifty years ago the reports by the Ford and Carnegie foundations in the United States argued for a more research and discipline-led focus (Gordon & Howell, 1959). The subsequent Porter and McKibbin report in the United States claimed that knowledge orientation had gone too far at the expense of practice — 'Business/management schools represent both an area of knowledge and a professional area of practice', and emphasis needed to be on both. The authors argued for a strengthening of the clinical approach to the education of students, combining knowledge dissemination, research investigation and on-site implementation of advanced methods of management analysis and practice. They acclaimed the medical school model (Porter & McKibbin, 1988). The theme of 'professionalism' continues in a recently published book that challenges business schools in the United States for abandoning the original 'professional project' of the early schools: *From Higher Aims to Hired Hands: The Social Transformation of American Business Schools and the Unfulfilled Promises of Management as a Profession* (Khurana, 2007).

Another recently published critical appraisal of business schools is *The Business School and the Bottom Line* (Starkey & Tiratsoo, 2007). This UK publication acknowledges the significant role of business schools as components in higher education throughout the world, but their diagnosis as to what needs to be done for continued success is not necessarily more professionalization of management. Business schools need to be more society oriented and less business oriented. They see this being achieved by recognizing that the business of the business school is knowledge. In other words, Starkey and Tiratsoo are trying to promote a broader agenda for business schools that goes beyond the 'bottom line'. The difficulty with their diagnosis and solution is that while it is thought provoking it is impractical from the historical perspective. Schools are already paying heed to the needs of society through electives on social responsibility and business ethics, and this trend is being reinforced by the accrediting bodies. Any more major change in orientation of business schools will have to come from the combined leadership of multiple stakeholders (see Figure 5.1), and there is little evidence that this will materialize in the foreseeable future given the current impressive performance of business schools in general.

5.3. Overview of a Remarkable Story

The history of UK business and management education is a remarkable story. Compared to some of our competitors, particularly the United States, there was very little evidence of formal management education in the United Kingdom prior to the early 1960s. Seeds had been tentatively sown in the first half of the past century by the introduction of isolated courses in some universities (e.g. Manchester) and by the pioneering efforts of a few outstanding individuals (e.g. Lyndal Urwick). It was left to the crises generated by the Second World War to awaken the need for management education among senior industrialists and politicians. Even then it was (a) non-university institutions (e.g. Henley and Ashridge) and (b) technical colleges and polytechnics (e.g. Regent Street Poly) that were keen to respond to this developing market. The traditional attitudes of academics questioned the academic basis of 'business and management'; and the traditional attitudes of industrialists questioned the value of theory to the practicalities of business and management. The breakthrough for both 'parties' emerged when sufficient forces combined to change these mental sets. The model of American business schools began to be seen as a means of improving the productivity of British industry. Hence the recommendations of a NEDC Report (NEDC, 1963), the Robbins Report (Robbins, 1963) and of course the Franks Report (Franks, 1963) for the establishment of one or two major business schools to rival the best in the United States.

With the anticipated launch of LBS and MBS, the establishment of management departments or business schools in the former CATs quickly followed (e.g. Cass, Bath). Several of the newly created universities were also quick to meet the needs of this developing market (e.g. Warwick, Strathclyde, Lancaster). Longer established universities soon climbed on board (e.g. Durham, Leeds). By the 1970s and 1980s a business school industry had taken firm root in the United Kingdom, and continued to strengthen with positive market forces, the development of the bodies, described in earlier sections, to improve the quality of management education (e.g. EQUIS, AMBA) and to promote the value of business schools to the national economy (e.g. ABS).

UK business schools have grown significantly and with great success to the point where business and management education is the most popular subject to study at university. From the latest HESA data available in 2008, almost one in seven of all students were studying business and management (ABS, 2009). This represents over 300,000 individual students or 234,00 full-time equivalents at all levels of higher education from foundation degrees, through traditional three and four year undergraduate degrees, MBAs, specialist masters and doctoral programmes.

This student body has also changed dramatically and is increasingly international. There are students coming to the United Kingdom from over 200 countries. As befits the area of study in the global era, 30% of business and management students now come from outside the United Kingdom and 25% from outside the European Union.

In terms of research strength in breadth and depth, the recent RAE revealed that research judged as world class and internationally excellent is far more widespread than at any previous time; the combined faculty numbers at about 12,500 (9,914 full-time equivalent students (ftes)) are at their highest point since records began.

All universities now have recognizable business schools and they have invested heavily not only in faculty and staff but also in refurbishment and new state of the art buildings. According to ABS well over £500 million has been invested over the past year alone.

Whether this state of affairs is the zenith or a pointer to further success, only time will tell but if those individuals in the early pioneering schools, government and industry were to have predicted what success might have looked like 50 years later surely, current results would exceed even their wildest expectations. It is a great tribute to all of those who have been involved subsequently to take business and management education to the mainstream and become the jewel in the crown of UK higher education. As yet, the international standing of the business school industry in the United Kingdom may not be comparable to that in the United States with its much longer history and its far larger industry. But on the basis of some of the evidence presented in Chapter 4 the United Kingdom is holding its own relative to other high-performing European countries (e.g. France and Spain), and is well ahead of non-European countries.

References

ABS. (2009). *Pillars of the sustainable economy: Sustainability and current market realities 2008/09*. London: ABS.

Antunes, D., & Thomas, H. (2007). The competitive (dis)advantages of European Business Schools. *Long Range Planning, 40*, 382–404.

Appleby, B. (1972). Papers on social science utilisation: Monograph 1. Centre for Utilisation of Social Science Research. Loughborough University of Technology, Loughborough, UK.

Ashton, D., & Gosling, J. (1991). *New models of advanced management education for experienced students. A view from abroad*. Miami Beach, FL: American Academy of Management.

Baillieu, C. (1945). *The Baillieu report*. London: Board of Trade.

Bain, G. (1993). *Commission on management research*. Swindon: ESRC.

Barnes, W. (1989). *Managerial Catalyst: The story of London Business School, 1964–1989*. London: Paul Chapman.

Belbin, M. (1981). *Management teams: Why they succeed or fail*. London: Butterworth-Heinemann.

Blain, I. (Ed.) (1971). *Occupational psychology: Jubilee volume*. London: NIIP.

Blake, R., & Mouton, J. (1964). *The managerial grid*. Houston, TX: Gulf Publishing.

Bradford, L., Gibb, J. et al. (Eds). (1964). *T-group theory and laboratory method*. New York: Wiley.

Bradley, L., Gregson, G., et al. (2004). *The challenge of business-university collaboration: Context, content and process*. London: Advanced Institute of Management.

Bradshaw, D. (2007). Business school rankings: The love-hate relationship. *Journal of Management Development, 26*(1), 54–60.

Brech, E. (2002). *The evolution of modern management: 1852–1979*. Bristol: Thoemmes Press.

Brech, E. F. L. (2000). *The evolution of modern management: For Britain, a two-century scenario*. Manuscript compiled for Open University Business School. London: p. 75.

Brodie, M. B. (1963). *On thinking statistically*. London: Hutchinson.

Brown, M. (1969). *The manager's guide to the behavioural sciences*. London: The Industrial Society.

Bruneel, J., D'Este, P., et al. (2009). *The search for talent and technology*. London: Advanced Institute of Management.

Burgoyne, J. (1988). *Competency based approach to management development*. Lancaster: Centre for the Study of Management Learning.

Burns, T., & Stalker, G. M. (1961). *The management of innovation*. London: Tavistock.

Cannon, T., & Taylor, F. (1994). *Management development in the millennium*. London: Institute of Management.

Caswill, C., & Wensley, R. (2007). Doors and boundaries: A recent history of the relationship between research and practice in UK organisational and management research. *Business History, 49*(3), 293–320.

CEML. (2002a). *The contributions of the UK business schools to developing managers and leaders: Report of the Business Schools Advisory Group*. Council for Excellence in Management and Leadership.

CEML. (2002b). *Managers and leaders: Raising our game*. London: Council for Excellence in Management and Leadership.

Chapman, J., Conlon, G., et al. (2008). *An economic impact assessment of the CCPMO*. London: London Economics.

Cherns, A. (1979). *Using the social sciences*. London: Routledge.

Child, J. (1969). *Brtish management thought*. London: Allen & Unwin.

Christensen, C. R. (1987). *Teaching and the case method*. Boston, MA: Harvard Business Press.

CIME, & ABS. (2006). *UK National Forum for Employers and Business School Deans*. London: Council for Industry and Higher Education.

CMI. (2008). *Management futures: The world in 2018* (pp. 1–25). London: Chartered Management Institute.

CNAA. (1989–1990). *Directory of CNAA first degree and undergraduate courses*. London: CNAA.

Constable, J., & McCormick, R. (1987). *The making of British managers*. London: BIM/CBI.

Coult, D. (1980). *A prospect of Ashridge*. Chichester: Phillimore.

Crick, W. F. (1964). *A higher award in business studies: Report of the advisory sub-committee on a higher award in business studies* (Ministry of Education). London: HMSO.

Cummings, S., & Daellenbach, U. (2009). A guide to the future of strategy? The history of Long Range Planning. *Long Range Planning, 42*(2), 234–263.

Dahrendorf, R. (1995). *A history of the London School of Economics and Political Science 1895–1995*. Oxford: Oxford University Press.

Davies, J., & Kelly, J. (1994). Partnership and complex relationships between business and education. *British Academy of Management Annual Conference*. September, Lancaster University, Lancaster, UK.

Dobbins, R., & Pettman, B. (2002). *What self-made millionaires really think, know and do*. Chichester: Capstone (Wiley).

Emery, F., & Trist, E. (1965). The causal texture of organisational environments. *Human Relations, 18*, 21–32.

Emery, F. E., & Trist, E. L. (1960). Socio-technical systems. In: C. W. Churchman & M. Verhulst (Eds), *Management sciences: Models and techniques* (Vol. 2). London: Pergamon.

Fayol, H. (1949). *General and industrial management* (C. Storrs, Trans. – from the original Administration Industrielle et Generale, 1916). London: Pitman.

Festinger, L. (1957). *A theory of cognitive dissonance*. Evanston, IL: Row Peterson.

Follett, M. P. (1920). *The new state*. London: Longmans, Green.

Foy, N. (1978). *The missing links: British management education in the eighties*. Oxford: Oxford Centre for Management Studies.

Franks, L. (1963). *British business schools*. London: HMSO.

Frisby, C. B. (1971). The development of industrial psychology at the NIIP: Some publications of the NIIP and its staff. In: I. Blain (Ed.), *Occupational psychology: Jubilee volume* (44, pp. 35–62). London: NIIP.

Gaither, N. (1986). Historical development of operations research (1940–1960). In: D. A. Wren (Ed.), *Papers dedicated to the development of modern management: Celebrating 100 years of modern management*. New York: The Academy of Management.

Gordon, R., & Howell, J. (1959). *Higher education in business*. New York: Columbia University Press.

Gourlay, D. (2005). *A history of Aberdeen business school 1965–2005*. Aberdeen: September.

Greensted, C. (2000). Measure for measure or a pound of flesh? (A comparison of quality assurance schemes). *International Journal of Management Education, 1*(1), 3–10.

Griffiths, B., & Murray, H. (1985). Whose business? A radical proposal to privatise British Business Schools. Hobart Paper. Institute of Economic Affairs, London.

Hale, E. (1964). *Report of the committee on university teaching methods*. London: HMSO, University Grants Committee.

Handy, C., Gordon, C., et al. (1987). *The making of managers*. London: NDEC/MSC/BIM.

Harte, N. (1986). *The university of London 1836–1986*. London: The Athlone Press.

Hewins, W. (1901). *Brief description of the objects and work of the school*. London: LSE.

Heyworth, L. (1965). *Report of the committee on social studies*. London: HMSO, Department of Education and Science.

Hull. (2009). *Origins and development of Hull University Business School*. Hull: ABS.

IM. (1994). *Management development to the Millennium: The Cannon and Taylor working party reports*. Institute of Management, London.

Ivory, C., Miskell, P., et al. (2006). *The future of business schools in the UK: Finding a path to success*. London: AIM.

Ivory, C., Miskell, P., et al. (2008). *Leadership of business schools: Perceptions, priorities and predicaments*. London: AIM.

Jarratt, S. A., Chairman. (1985). *Steering committee for efficiency studies in universities*. Report. CVCP, London.

Judge. (2009). *The first twenty years: A celebration*. Cambridge: Judge Business School.

Kempner, T. (Ed.) (1971). *The handbook of management*. London: Weidenfeld & Nicolson.

Khurana, R. (2007). *From higher aims to hired hands: The social transformation of American Business Schools and the unfulfilled promises of management as a profession*. Princeton: Princeton University Press.

Kolb, D. (1984). *Experiential learning: Experience as the source of learning and development*. Englewood Cliffs, NJ: Prentice-Hall.

Larson, M. J. (2009). *The federation of British Industry and Management Education in post-war Britain*. Cardiff Historical Papers, pp. 1–32. Cardiff University, Cardiff, UK.

Leitch, L. (2006). *Leitch review of skills*. London: HM Treasury.

Lewin, K. (1951). *Field theory in social science*. New York: Harper and Row.

Livy, B. (Ed.) (1980). *Management and people in banking*. London: IOB.

Loveridge, R., Willman, P., et al. (2007). 60 years of human relations. *Human Relations, 60*(12), 1873–1888.

Lupton, T. (1966). *Management and the Social sciences*. London: Penguin.

Mabey, C., & Ramirez, M. (2004). *Developing managers: A European perspective*. London: Chartered Management Institute.

Mace, C. A. (1952). Education for management in the United States: Some impressions and reflections. *Occupational Psychology, 26*(2), 61–69.

Mansfield, R. (2010). *Cardiff Business School*. Unpublished paper. Cardiff Business School, Cardiff, UK.

Matthews, D., Anderson, M., et al. (1997). The rise of the professional accountant in British management. *The Economic History Review, 50*(3), 407–429.

McGregor, D. (1960). *The human side of enterprise*. New York: McGraw-Hill.

McKiernan, P. (2008). *History of the British Academy of Management*. London: BAM.

Miles, D. (1996). *The development of management education*. The Second De Lissa Lecture, pp. 1–19, London.

Mintzberg, H. (2004). *Managers not MBAs: A hard look at the soft practice of managing and management development*. London: FT Prentice Hall.

Moore, S. (2007). Economic and social sciences since 1903. In: B. Pullan (Ed.), *A portrait of the University of Manchester*. London: Third Millennium Publishing.

Morris, H. (2010). Business and management research in the UK from 1900 to 2009. Unpublished paper. Manchester Metropolitan University, Manchester, UK.

Morris, J. (1977). Tacking down the middle: Ten years of OD by a British business school. In: C. L. Cooper (Ed.), *OD in the UK and the USA*. London: Macmillan.

Murphy, M. (1953). Education for management in Great Britain. *The Journal of Business of the University of Chicago, 26*(1), 37–47.

Muscio, B. (1920). *Lectures on Industrial Administration*. London: Routledge.

Myers, C. (1920). Psychology and industry. *British Journal of Psychology, 10*, 177–182.

NEDC (1963). *Management education?* London: NEDC.

Nind, P. (1985). *A firm foundation: The story of the foundation for management education*. London: FME.

Owen, T. (1970). *Business schools: The requirements of British manufacturing industry*. London: BIM.

Pedler, M., Burgoyne, J., et al. (1991). *The learning company: A strategy for sustainable development*. London: McGraw-Hill.

Platt J. W. (1968). *Education for management: A review of the diploma in management.* London: Foundation for Management Education.

Porter, L., & McKibbin, L. (1988). *Management education and development drift or thrust into the 21 century.* New York: McGraw-Hill.

Pugh, D. (Ed.) (1966). *The academic teaching of management.* ATM Occasional Papers. London.

Pugh, D., & Hickson, D. (2007). *Great writers on organisations: The third omnibus edition.* Abingdon: Ashgate.

Pugh, D. S. (1996). A taste for innovation. In: *Management laureates* (Vol. 4, pp. 235–276). Stamford, CT: JAI Press Inc.

Pugh, D. S., Hickson, D. J., et al. (1964). *Writers on organizations: An introduction.* London: Hutchinson.

Raphael, W. (1971). NIIP and its staff 1921 to 1961. In: I. J. Blain (Ed.), *Occupational psychology: Jubilee volume.* London: NIIP.

Revans, R. (1978). *The ABC of action learning: A review of 25 years of experience.* Altrincham, Manchester: R.W. Revans.

Rice, A. K., Hill, J. M., et al. (1950). The representation of labour turnover as a social process: Studies in the social development of an industrial community (the Glacier Project). *Human Relations, 3,* 349–372.

Robbins, L. (1963). *Report of the committee on higher education.* London: HMSO.

RoffeyPark (2006). *The story of Roffey Park: 1946–2006.* Roffey Park Management College, Roffey Park Internet Site.

Rose, H. (1970). *Management education in the 1970s.* London: HMSO.

RSA. (1995). *Tomorrow's company.* London: RSA.

Rundle, D. (2006). *Henley and the unfinished management education revolution.* Henley: Henley Management College.

Sanecki, K. (1996). *Ashridge: A living history.* Chichester: Phillimore.

Schein, E. H. (1985). *Organisational culture and leadership.* San Francisco, CA: Jossey-Bass.

Servan-Schreiber, S. (1994). *Les Epices de la Republique: ESCP Itinerire d'une grande ecole, 1819–1994.* Paris: CpL.

Shimmin, S., & Wallis, D. (1994). *Fifty years of occupational psychology in Britain.* Leicester: British Psychological Society.

Silverstone, R., & Williams, A. P. O. (1979). Recruitment, training, employment and careers of women chartered accountants in England and Wales. *Accounting and Business Research, 9*(34), 105–121.

Skinner, B. (1976). *About behaviourism.* New York: Vintage Books.

Skrovan, D. J. (Ed.) (1983). *Quality of work life: Perspectives for business and the public sector.* Reading: MA: Addison-Wesley.

Slater, H. (1989). *Henley at Greenlands: Forty years of management development.* Henley-on-Thames: Henley Management College.

Starkey, K., & Madan, P. (2001). Bridging the relevance gap: Aligning stakeholders in the future of management research. *British Journal of Management, 12*(Special Issue), S3–S26.

Starkey, K., & Tiratsoo, N. (2007). *The business school and the bottom line.* Cambridge: Cambridge University Press.

Starkey, K., & Tranfield, D. (1998). The nature, social organisation and promotion of management research: towards policy. *British Journal of Management, 9,* 341–353.

Stewart, R. (1963). *The Reality of Management.* London: William Heinemann Ltd.

Taylor, F. W. (1903). *Shop management.* New York: Harper.

Taylor, F. W. (1911). *Principles of scientific management.* London: Harper.

Taylor, R. (2007). *The history of chambers of commerce in the UK: 1768–2007.* London: The British Chambers of Commerce.

Teare, R., & Prestoungrange, G. (2004). *Accrediting managers at work in the 21st century.* Prestonpans, Scotland: Prestoungrange University Press.

Teeling, S., & Filby, J. (2008). *Aston business school: 1947/48–2007/08.* Birmingham: Aston Business School.

Thomas, H. (2007). An analysis of the environment and competitive dynamics of management education. *Journal of Management Development, 26*(1), 9–21.

Thomasen, J. (2009). *Ashridge.* Berkhamsted: Ashridge.

Torrington, D. (2002). *Manchester school of management 1918–2000: A collective memory.* Manchester: Manchester School of Management, UMIST.

Trapnell, J. (2007). AACSB international accreditation: The value proposition and a look to the future. *Journal of Management Development, 26*(1), 67–72.

Trist, E., & Bamforth, K. (1951). Some social and psychological consequences of the longwall method of coal-getting: An examination of the psychological situation and defences of a work group in relation to the social structure and technological content of the work system. *Human Relations, 4,* 3–38.

Trist, E. L., Higgin, G. W., Murray, H., & Pollock, A. B. (1963). *Organisational choice.* London: Tavistock.

Tweedale, G., & Hansen, P. (2000). *Magic mineral to killer dust: Turner & Newall and the asbestos hazard.* Oxford: Oxford University Press.

Urgel, J. (2007). EQUIS accreditation: Value and benefits for international business schools. *Journal of Management Development, 26*(1), 73–83.

Urwick, L. (1947). *Education for management: Management subjects in technical and commercial colleges.* Report of a special committee appointed by the Minister of Education. Ministry of Education, London.

Urwick, L. F., & Brech, E. F. L. (1946). *The making of scientific management.* London: Management Publications Trust.

WBS. (2007). *Warwick Business School: Building on 40 years of innovation, diversity, and success.* Warwick: Warwick Business School.

Welch, H. J., & Myers, C. S. (1932). *Ten years of industrial psychology: An account of the first decade of NIIP.* London: Pitman.

Whitaker, G. (Ed.) (1965). *T-group Training: group dynamics in management education.* ATM Occasional Papers. Blackwell, Oxford.

Wilde. (1973). *The Institute of Bankers educational policy review.* A report by the Wilde Committee. IOB, London.

Williams, A. P. O. (1974). Beyond academic respectability. *Quest: The Journal of City University London, 12,* 30–33.

Williams, A. P. O. (1980). Integrating individual and organisational learning: A model and a case study. *Management Education and Development, 11*(1), 7–20.

Williams, A. P. O. (2001). A belief-focused model of organisational learning. *Journal of Management Studies, 38*(1), 67–85.

Williams, A. P. O. (2006). *The rise of Cass Business School: The journey to world-class, 1966 onwards.* Basingstoke: Palgrave Macmillan.

Williams, A. P. O. (2007). *The fifteenth anniversary of ABS: 1992–2007.* London: Association of Business Schools.

Williams, A. P. O., Dobson, P., et al. (1989). *Changing culture: New organisational approaches.* London: Institute of Personnel and Development.

Wilson, J., & Thomson, A. (2006). *The making of modern management: British management in historical perspective.* Oxford: Oxford University Press.

Wilson, J. F. (1992). *The Manchester experiment: A history of Manchester Business School 1965–1990.* London: Paul Chapman.

Wilton, P., Woodman, P., et al. (2007). *The value of management qualifications: The perspective of UK employers and managers* (pp. 1–24). London: Chartered Management Institute.

Witzel, M. (2009). *Management history: Text and cases.* London: Routledge.

Woodward, J. (1958). *Management and technology.* London: HMSO/DSIR.

Appendices

Appendix 1. Methodology and Acknowledgements

Methodology

The project was initiated by ABS after Professor Sir George Bain observed that a book was needed that would account for the rise of business and management education in the United Kingdom. The idea was that it should focus particularly on business schools. Emerald Group Publishing Ltd declared an interest in publishing the book on being approached by Howard Thomas on behalf of ABS. Discussions with the author took place in the first two months of 2009, and work commenced around Easter of that year. An important constraining factor was that the target date for publication was October 2010 in time for the AGM of ABS, which meant that a completed manuscript would need to be available by June of that year.

Inevitably the time factor had an influence on the strategy followed in researching and writing the book, although the focus on business schools in the United Kingdom did make the task more manageable. There were four phases to the project. The first was to learn what others had identified as significant influences in the development of management education in the United Kingdom. The second was to prepare a handout listing the milestones with appropriate dates. The handout included: (a) institutions involved in education and dissemination of knowledge relating to business and manage-ment in the United Kingdom and (b) authors and publications that had influenced the growth and content of business and management education in the United Kingdom. A number of individuals who had played important roles in the post-1960 period were interviewed in order to gauge the relative significance of items included, and to reveal gaps. The handout was revised in the light of new information gathered. Box 1.2 is the end product. The list covering authors and publications was dropped (except for 'reports') because of the difficulty in validating responses within the time available.

The third phase was exploring in more depth those items that seemed to be critical in the development of management education, and creating a structure (i.e. Chapters 1–4) that would aid the process of completing the task. The features of the structure emerged from the mass of data accumulated; in other words, it was the one that 'made sense' to the author. The fourth phase was drafting out, and continually revising the history in the light of further information and useful feedback. Besides interviews and publications, a useful source of information was the Internet; particularly true in the context of professional associations. Members of ABS were invited to send any material they had on the history of their school. Unfortunately few were able to respond positively with in-depth histories; those that did will be evident from the references.

Acknowledgements

Researching a theme such as the history of UK business and management education is going to depend upon the earlier scholarship of others and the current co-operation of many individuals. The list of references recognizes the contribution of the former, but it remains to highlight a number of individuals who have been most helpful through interviews and emails. They include (in no particular order): Professors Andrew Thomson, Angela Bowey, Derek Pugh, Philip Sadler, David Miles, Howard Thomas, David Wilson, Huw Morris, Roger Mansfield, Peter McKiernan, Robin Wensley, Val Hammond, Mike Jones. I am grateful to all of them, and to those who responded to Jonathan Slack's call for written histories of their business school. A particular thanks to Huw Morris, Howard Thomas, Derek Pugh and Jonathan Slack who read earlier drafts of the manuscript and provided helpful comments and suggestions. In addition, Huw and Howard must be thanked for writing a most informative Foreword, and Jonathan for his readiness to provide help as the need arose.

Many thanks must also go to the representatives of Emerald Press for their helpful and enthusiastic co-operation in the process of preparing the publication. Lastly grateful thanks to Sally Helper of the British Library for kindly instructing me on how to make best use of its resources.

Appendix 2.   ABS Members as of March 2010

Aberdeen Business School, The Robert Gordon University
University of Aberdeen Business School
School of Management and Business, Aberystwyth University
Ashcroft International Business School, Anglia Ruskin University

Ashridge Business School
Aston Business School, Aston University
Bangor Business School, Bangor University
School of Management, University of Bath
University of Bedfordshire Business School
Birmingham Business School, University of Birmingham
Birmingham City Business School, Birmingham City University
Bolton Business School, University of Bolton
Bournemouth University Business School
Bradford University School of Management
Brighton Business School, University of Brighton
Bristol Business School, University of the West of England
Department of Management, University of Bristol
Brunel Business School, Brunel University
University of Buckingham Business School
School of Business and Management, Buckinghamshire New University
Canterbury Christchurch University, Faculty of Business & Management
Cardiff Business School, Cardiff University
Cardiff School of Management, University of Wales Institute, Cardiff
Cass Business School, City University London
Faculty of Business, Enterprise and Lifelong Learning, University of Chester
Coventry Business School, Coventry University
Cranfield School of Management
Croydon College, Department of Management
Cumbria Business School, University of Cumbria
Derbyshire Business School, University of Derby
Dundee Business School, University of Abertay Dundee
Durham Business School, Durham University
University of East London Royal Docks Business School
Edge Hill University, Business School
University of Edinburgh Business School
Edinburgh Napier University Business School
ESCP Europe
Essex Business School, University of Essex
European Business School London, Regent's College
University of Exeter Business School
Glamorgan Business School, University of Glamorgan
University of Glasgow Business School
Caledonian Business School, Glasgow Caledonian University
University of Gloucestershire Business School
University of Greenwich Business School
Henley Business School, University of Reading
School of Management and Languages, Heriot-Watt University

University of Hertfordshire Business School
University of Huddersfield Business School
Hull University Business School, University of Hull
Imperial College Business School
Judge Business School, University of Cambridge
Keele Management School, Keele University
Kent Business School, University of Kent
Kingston Business School, Kingston University
Lancashire Business School, University of Central Lancashire
Lancaster University Management School
Leeds Business School, Leeds Metropolitan University
Leeds University Business School, University of Leeds
Leicester Business School, De Montfort University
University of Leicester School of Management
Lincoln Business School, University of Lincoln
Liverpool Business School, Liverpool John Moores University
Liverpool Hope University College, Management and Business
University of Liverpool Management School
London Business School
School of Management and Science, London College of Fashion
London Metropolitan Business School, London Metropolitan University
Faculty of Business, London South Bank University
Loughborough University Business School
Manchester Business School, University of Manchester
Manchester Metropolitan University Business School
Middlesex University Business School
Newcastle Business School, Northumbria University
Newcastle University Business School
Newport Business School, University of Wales, Newport
Northampton Business School, The University of Northampton
Norwich Business School, University of East Anglia
Nottingham Business School, Nottingham Trent University
Nottingham University Business School
Open University Business School
Oxford Brookes University Business School
Plymouth Business School, University of Plymouth
Portsmouth Business School, University of Portsmouth
School of Business and Management, Queen Mary University, London
Queen's University Management School, Queen's University Belfast
Regent's Business School London, Regent's College
School of Business and Social Sciences, Roehampton University
School of Business and Management, Royal Agricultural College
School of Management, Royal Holloway, University of London

Saïd Business School, University of Oxford
Salford Business School, University of Salford
Sheffield Business School, Sheffield Hallam University
The University of Sheffield Management School
Southampton Business School, Southampton Solent University
University of Southampton School of Management
Staffordshire University Business School
School of Management, University of St. Andrews
Stirling Management School, University of Stirling
Strathclyde Business School, University of Strathclyde
Sunderland Business School, University of Sunderland
School of Management, University of Surrey
University of Sussex, Science and Technology Policy Research (SPRU)
Swansea Business School, Swansea Metropolitan University
School of Business and Economics, Swansea University
Teesside Business School, University of Teesside
Thames Valley University Business School
Ulster Business School, University of Ulster
Warwick Business School, University of Warwick
University of the West of Scotland Business School
Westminster Business School, University of Westminster
Winchester Business School, University of Winchester
University of Wolverhampton Business School
Worcester Business School, University of Worcester
Wrexham Business School, Glyndŵr University
York St John Business School, York St John University

Associated Organizations
Association of Graduate Recruiters (AGR)
Association of MBAs
Bath Spa University College
Business, Management, Accountancy and Finance (BMAF) Subject Centre
Chartered Institute of Marketing
Chartered Institute of Personnel and Development
Chartered Institute of Public Relations
Chartered Management Institute
European Foundation for Management Development (EFMD)
ifs School of Finance
Isle of Man International Business School

Subject Index

Academics

Consultancies

Educational institutions
Business schools

Learned Societies

Learning methods & Programmes

Professional bodies & Regulators

Theories & Concepts

About the Author

Allan P. O. Williams is an Emeritus Professor at Cass Business School, City University London. After studying psychology at Manchester University and occupational psychology at Birkbeck College, he researched in the emerging field of teaching machines and programmed learning in the late 1950s. He then spent three years in market research developing new techniques for evaluating the visual impact of packaging and advertising. He was recruited in 1963 to help develop management education at the Northampton College of Advanced Technology, which became City University in 1966. His 38 years of employment at the University saw him take on various roles including: Head of Industrial Relations and Personnel Management; Director of the Centre for Personnel Research and Enterprise Development; Head of Business Studies Department; Deputy Dean of the Business School; Pro-Vice-Chancellor of the University. He has been an Officer of the British Psychological Society, and served on professional and scientific bodies such as the Board of Directors of the International Association of Applied Psychology, the Council of the British Academy of Management, the Medical Research Council's Army Personnel Research Committee. He has served for many years on Civil Service Selection Boards and charitable Trusts. He is a Founder Liveryman of the Worshipful Company of Management Consultants, Fellow of the British Psychological Society, the International Association of Applied Psychology and the British Academy of Management, and Academician of the Academy of Social Sciences. His publications relate mainly to HRM and organization development, and more recently to leadership and organizational histories.